MW00992739

The Difference is in the
Dispensations
How to Make Sense of the Differences in the Bible

Timothy S. Morton

Morton Publications
2101 Morton Road
Sutton, WV 26601

www.preservedwords.com

Other works by this author,

More Than Forgiven
Which Translation Should You Trust
From Marriage to Remarriage
From Liberty to Legalism
Top Taboo Topics

Contents

Introduction...1

Chapter I
The Covenants and The Dispensations.............................5
The Edenic Covenant and The Dispensation of Innocence..........6
The Adamic Covenant and The Dispensation of Conscience.......8
The Noahic Covenant and The Dispensation of Human Gov....12
Rebellion at Babel..13
The Abrahamic Covenant and The Dispensation of Promise....16
The Mosaic Covenant and The Dispensation of the Law...........18
The Davidic Covenant and The Dispensation of Grace.............21
The Tribulation Period..25
The Palestinian and New Covenant and The Messianic Disp....26
The New Heavens, The New Earth, and The New Jerusalem...30
The Great Lesson...32

Chapter II
Salvation In The Old Testament.......................................34
Innocent Adam...37
Cain and Abel..42
Noah and the Ark..44
Faithful Abraham..45
Abraham's Seed..47
Moses the Law Giver...49
Aaron..53
Samson..55
Saul..56
Joab..57
David...58

Chapter III
Salvation In The New Testament......................................62
The Old Testament In The New...64
Examining Matthew...67

The New Birth..71
From Law To Grace...73
Unraveling Acts..74
Cornelius...78
The Disciples Meet..81

Chapter IV
Salvation In The New Testament cont...........................83
How Many Gospels?...83
Understanding Hebrews...85
James...91
Salvation in the Tribulation..92
The Millennium And Beyond...96
The New Heavens And New Earth.................................99
A Final Word...101
A Dispensational Chart..103

Introduction

When a person receives the Lord Jesus Christ as his Savior, he, with the Lord, also receives a desire to know more about his salvation and the one who saved him (John 15:26). This desire causes the new believer, possibly for the very first time in his life, to open the Holy Bible in a serious attempt to learn what God has to say. Once in the Scriptures the believer soon realizes that the Bible speaks of much more than just personal salvation and Christ dying on the cross; it speaks of God's *whole program* for His entire creation from eternity to eternity. It reveals what God wants man to know about *God Himself, His creation,* and *His purpose with His creation.* Unless the believer understands this and divides the Bible accordingly (2 Tim. 2:15), he may become overwhelmed by its vast scope and perplexed by its differences. All the Bible's major differences can be reconciled with some study (sometimes very little), but if the believer neglects to study and sort these differences out, he will cheat himself out of understanding not only God's plan and purpose for man in general, but also for himself in particular.

However, even though the Bible is in some areas complex and interwoven, one notable indication that it is the very word of God is the most *vital* and *important subjects* found in it are easy to understand. God has purposely made the crucial subjects of *sin, man's accountability to God, Christ's substitutionary death, and personal salvation* so simple a small child can understand them. He made these matters clear and easy to comprehend so any person wanting the truth about them could by faith act upon them and receive the Lord Jesus Christ as his salvation. These clear yet vital doctrines are referred to as the **"simplicity that is in Christ"** (2 Cor. 11:3). Though the more complex subjects reveal more of the mind and intentions of God, knowledge of them is not necessary for one to be saved.

Needless to say, the Bible contains both simplicity and complexity by God's direction. He wanted to provide a salvation so simple that a person could understand it and get saved after only being presented with the gospel *once* (Acts 10:43-44, 16:31, etc.), but He also wanted some other matters more detailed and complex so one would have to labor in the Scriptures a certain degree to sort them out. In this respect some Bible subjects are so mysterious and far-ranging in their scope that no one yet has done much more than scratch the surface of the treasures within them, let alone fully grasp them. Sometimes the Lord even spoke in **"parables"** to purposely confound those who listen to His words with the wrong **"heart"** or attitude: those who don't have **"ears to hear"** (Matt. 13:9-15).

If a person reads the Bible very much at all he is soon confronted with various *laws, judgments, ordinances, commandments, doctrines, kingdoms, covenants, testaments, dispensations, gospels, priesthoods, feasts, tribes, churches,* etc., and begins to see some of the Bible's complexity. He is further introduced to events known as the *Exodus, Israel's Captivity, Daniel's Seventieth Week, the Rapture, the Judgment Seat of Christ, the Tribulation, the Millennium, the White Throne Judgment, the New Heaven and New Earth, etc.,* that add even more to its broad variety of topics.

Once a reader gets to this point questions usually arise: Where do all these subjects belong? Do they all apply to everyone in every age? Does every precept mentioned in the Bible apply doctrinally to a Christian? What about the doctrines that appear to contradict each other? Is salvation *exactly* the same in every age? How is one to account for the differences? With this book we will show that the major differences in the Bible can be reconciled by rightly dividing it into *dispensations* and keeping the different doctrines found in the dispensations in their proper place.

In 2 Timothy 2:15 the Holy Spirit states His word has divisions and the **"workman"** must **"study"** to **"rightly"** divide them. When a believer obeys God's word and with study finds these divisions and applies the truths found in them to their proper place, much of the Bible's complexity disappears and many of its alleged contradictions vanish. Furthermore, many of the different manners, methods, and doctrines in the Bible which often trouble people are reconciled, and the believer begins to see the "big picture" of what God is doing.

Since properly understanding the Bible's divisions is the key to being sound in doctrine and making sense of its differences, failure to do so can lead to dangerous heresies and spiritual chaos. When a preacher or any other believer fails to rightly divide the Bible and discern its differences, he will nearly always end up wresting it. This is one reason there are so many "Christian" cults today. Instead of rightly dividing the Bible, they ignore some or all of its divisions and produce a religious system that is littered with heresies, some of them *deadly*. When a person takes a precept or doctrine peculiar to one dispensation and forces it to apply doctrinally to another, he ends up with a heresy every time. He may quote several Bible verses to "prove" his doctrine, but it is still a lie once it is divorced from its corresponding dispensation.

In view of this, it is essential that every believer keep in mind that God spoke the words recorded in the Bible in **"sundry times and diverse manners"** (Heb. 1:1): to different people at different times. Thus the Scriptures were not written only for believers in the present Church Age, they were written for believers (and unbelievers) of all the ages. In short, the Bible was written FOR everyone for their learning (Rom. 15:4) but not addressed TO everyone in every age for doctrine. True, every verse in the Bible applies doctrinally *somewhere,* but many verses found in it do not apply doctrinally today. Of course, any Bible passage can be used *inspirationally* in any dispensation to help teach a present truth, but *doctrine* is another matter. For instance, most will agree the laws God gave to Israel through Moses do not apply doctrinally to Christians. The Israelites had strict religious, social, and dietary laws they had to comply with (Lev. ch. 1-15), but none of these laws, as laws, apply to believers today (Col. 2:14). A Jew at that time even had to have a human priest to work in his behalf towards God; today, every Christian is a priest himself (1 Peter 2:9). If one doesn't rightly divide the word of truth he can't help but wrest it, no matter how "sincere and devoted" he is.

Concerning the dividing of the Bible into dispensations, even the most liberal Bible readers (who often criticize "dispensationalism") will acknowledge at least one division in the Scriptures: the division between Malachi and Matthew dividing to Old from the New Testament. This division is so obvious that even an atheist can find it. Anyone who has read the Bible much at all knows the Old Testament is different from the New Testament and by doing so he admits to two dispensations. This makes him a "dispensationalist" whether he refers to himself as one or not. If these critics would study their Bibles a little more and believe what they read, they would find at least six more important divisions, each one revealing vital lessons.

A very large work would be required for one to try to exhaustively categorize and reconcile every difference found in the Bible, thus this is well beyond the scope of this relatively small book. The main purpose of this book is to present to the reader in a concise manner the principal and most important divisions of the Bible by examining its *covenants* and *dispensations*.

In addition, since the subject of *personal salvation* from sin is the most important and relevant issue to a sinner in any dispensation (and also probably the subject that causes the most debate and controversy among professing Christians today), we will also look at the dispensations from this perspective. In the first chapter we will briefly examine each covenant and its accompanying dispensation, noting the major elements of each; then in the following chapters we will take on the crucial subject of personal salvation in the different dispensations and examine the differences between them in this context.

Chapter I
The Covenants and The Dispensations

Over the centuries believers have developed several methods of studying the Bible. Some study it *systematically* by topic, others use an *inductive* or *deductive* method to arrive at conclusions, still others divide the Bible into *"stages"* or sections to make it more manageable, many study guides *outline* studies by book, chapter, or topic, and yet others study it dispensationally. Although there is merit in all of these methods, studying the Bible dispensationally with the covenants marking the divisions is the easiest and surest way one can see the various systems God has placed in the Scriptures and get a sufficient understanding of what He is doing. The Bible's divisions do not neatly divide between books, chapters, or subjective "stages," so the best method to get the overall picture of God's program is to study the Bible using its own terms of **"covenant"** and **"dispensation,"** letting them mark the divisions.

Defining the Terms

A covenant is generally defined as a *mutual agreement between two parties.* In the Scriptures some covenants are unconditional and continue regardless of the conduct of man, while others are conditioned on obedience. Each covenant God makes with man (with few exceptions) marks the beginning of a new dispensation. The dispensation carries on the doctrines God established with the covenant.

Another word for covenant in the Bible is **"testament,"** thus the 27 books known as the New Testament proclaim the new covenant God has made with man through the blood of the Lord Jesus Christ. Technically, much of the first four books of the New Testament (the gospels) refer to events that occurred under the old covenant of the Law, but the atonement Christ made with his death and resurrection as revealed in the gospels made possible the new covenant of grace in effect today.

5

A dispensation is usually defined as a "period of time" in which God works with and in His people in a particular way, but this is only partially true. Calling a dispensation primarily a period of time will not bear up under close scrutiny of the Scriptures. In the Bible the term "dispensation" refers to a *manner, method, or particular arrangement of dealing with people God has chosen to dispense during a period of time*, not the time period itself. Usually the length of time is not emphasized or even mentioned, it is the doctrines God has established to be valid during that time that distinguishes one dispensation from another. In short, a dispensation is a certain *mode of testing* God has dispensed to man, while a covenant is a *contract or promise* between God and man.

The term **"dispensation"** is found four times in the Scriptures (1 Cor. 9:17; Eph. 1:10, 3:2; Col. 1:25), and each passage makes it clear that God is dispensing something. In Eph. 3:2 it is **"grace"** itself that is dispensed, not a period of time called the "grace of God." God revealed through Paul how He was dispensing His grace to all men by making a free salvation available to them in Jesus Christ. This is contrasted with the *Dispensation of the Law* where God gave mainly law (though grace can be readily found in every dispensation). Under the Law obedience was demanded, obey the laws and live; break them and die (Gal. 3:10-13). In this Church Age of Grace, however, it is not obey the law but only receive Christ to be saved. In a nutshell, God simply uses covenants and dispensations to deal with man in different manners under different circumstances to teach and show him things about himself and his Creator.

The Edenic Covenant and The Dispensation of Innocence

Obviously, all things begin with God, and God's dealings with man began the moment He created Adam. Genesis chapters 1-3 tell us God didn't create Adam to only lounge in a beautiful garden, He gave him specific commands to obey and jobs to occupy him. This contract between God and Adam is the first covenant between God and any man; it is commonly known as the Edenic Covenant. In this covenant God supplied Adam with many blessings, among them *life, a perfect body, a perfect environment, a world without pain, hunger, sickness or death, and also a wife.* All Adam (and Eve) had to do was to keep six conditions God had laid down to keep the covenant in effect with all its blessings. God told them to:

- Multiply and replenish the earth (Gen. 1:28).
- Subdue the earth for their use (Gen. 1:28).
- Exercise dominion over the animal creation (Gen. 1:28).
- Have only a vegetable diet (Gen. 1:29).
- Dress and keep the garden they were put in (Gen. 2:15).
- Abstain from eating from the Tree of Knowledge of Good and Evil (Gen. 2:17).

This covenant remained in force until Adam broke it by eating of the forbidden tree. God kept his part but man did not keep his. A trend that will sadly continue through every dispensation.

The *Edenic Covenant* introduced the *Dispensation of Innocence*. The doctrines or requirements God established with the *Edenic Covenant* (above) expressed the kind of behavior He desired from Adam while it was in force. Remember, a covenant is an agreement or contract between God and man, it may be conditional (as this covenant) or unconditional. On the other hand a dispensation is the particular method of dealing WITH man God works under (the doctrines He has dispensed to be valid during that time), and the manner of behavior He requires OF man during the time period which began with a covenant.

The *Dispensation of Innocence* is so named because Adam was created as an innocent creature and had no natural inclination towards evil or righteousness. Although Adam was not a "sinner" until he ate of the tree of knowledge, neither was he righteous in God's sight. He was merely an innocent, untested creature who had no evil in him to separate him from God, nor any righteousness in him to commend him to God. Before he fell Adam was in a kind of moral "limbo" which God apparently never intended him to stay in long.

Some believers mistakenly believe the condition Adam was in at creation is the position a born again believer has before God in this present dispensation. They think salvation only puts them back like Adam was before the fall; that is, in an innocent state. If this were true a Christian could lose his salvation! Adam fell from his innocent position! This is a good example of failure to properly divide the Scriptures, and the Christians who hold this view are robbing themselves of some of the most precious truths concerning New Testament salvation. More on this later.

With this case of Adam alone we can already see how dispensations differ from each other. There is very little the *Dispensation of Innocence* has in common with any other dispensation. Nowhere in the dispensations of *Family, Law, Grace, etc.*, does God command anyone to *subdue the earth, keep a garden, eat only vegetables, or not eat of a certain tree.* These doctrines were valid ONLY as long as the covenant and following dispensation were in force. When Adam broke the covenant, its doctrines were superseded by the next one.

When Adam ate of the Tree of Knowledge he died spiritually (Eph.2:1) and acquired an evil nature, but God in an act of mercy and grace did not yet allow him to die physically. His body did begin on its trek toward the grave, but God quickly made another covenant with Adam which contained a promise of ultimate deliverance.

The Adamic Covenant and The Dispensation of Conscience

When Adam ate of the forbidden tree at the bidding of his wife, they both acquired something they before thought desirable but soon turned out to be a curse; that is, knowledge. After Adam ate they both quickly learned the knowledge they obtained was quite different from what the Serpent represented it to be. It was not just "knowledge" for knowledge's sake, but the *knowledge of EVIL.* Contrary to many not all knowledge is beneficial. There are some things a person should not try to learn or seek after, and the greatest of these is a knowledge of evil (Rom. 16:19; 1 Co. 14:20). It is the knowledge of evil that condemned Adam and Eve to death, and it is the same that separates one child who is accountable for his actions from another who is not. In fact, it is the knowledge of evil or sin that condemns every man as a sinner, and every person born of Adam inherits the capacity for this knowledge. That the Serpent deceived Eve and led her to think all knowledge was desirable is immaterial. Adam knew exactly what God said; he made his choice for Eve knowing they both would die (1 Tim 2:14).

After he ate, Adam knew at least three things he didn't know before. He knew he had eaten of the forbidden tree and would die; he knew he had broken God's covenant; and he knew he was naked. This new knowledge caused him to feel fear and guilt for the first time and these in turn caused him to flee from God's presence. In spite of Adam's blatant sin, God did not abandon him. Though the *Edenic Covenant* was now broken, God did not cast aside His new creation. By His foreknowledge and grace He made another covenant with Adam, and unlike the first one this covenant was unconditional and is still in effect today. It is called the *Adamic Covenant.*

Knowing the end from the beginning and the whole scheme of events He would allow to follow, God made such a far-ranging covenant with Adam, including all of his descendants, that it remains fully valid with its effects still felt today. This covenant testifies to all mankind the willing act of disobedience their father Adam performed in a garden so long ago. This covenant, given to Adam and Eve before they were expelled from the presence of the Tree of Life, is composed of several curses and a promise. The curses affect all three parties involved in the sin.

- The *Serpent,* which was the fleshy tool of Satan, was cursed to crawl upon the ground and eat dust (Gen. 3:14). This curse remains in effect through the Millennium (Isa. 65:25).

- As for the *woman,* she was to have multiplied conception. One reason for this is because the earth will be harder to fill with people with the entrance of death.
- She also was to bear children in sorrow. She is going to have more children but will have to bear them in sorrow because she is bringing another "sinner" into the world.
- Thirdly, the woman will have a desire for her husband and will be in subjection to him (Gen. 3:16).

- As for the *man,* first of all the ground that so freely gave forth its fruit was cursed. Man must now till the ground in sorrow and sweat and endure weeds that will choke and weaken his crops.

- Then, after a life of labor and toil, he must pay for his sin in the garden and physically die, returning to the earth he worked (Gen. 3:17-19).

Man has spent the last six millennia trying to undo everyone of these curses (with drugs, chemicals, technology, etc.) with only superficial success, but, of course, the curse he is most desperately trying to stop is *death*. Ever since Adam man has sought ways to overcome death or at least delay it for even a short period (Satan knows this well, Job 2:4), but eventually death wins out. The death rate remains 100%. God cannot be beaten, what He has cursed is cursed. These curses will not be completely lifted until the renovation of the earth by fire after the Millennium.

Among these sorrowful curses, however, God has thrown in a precious promise (Gen. 3:15). Its purpose was to show mankind what kind of God the Lord is and to show him He will provide a means of deliverance that can ultimately release him from the curses. The promise (which was actually addressed to the Serpent) was the **"seed"** of the woman (Christ) would bruise the head of the Serpent (a mortal blow) while the seed of the Serpent (the Beast) will bruise the woman's seed's heel. To Adam (and to those many centuries after him) this likely meant that a future **"seed,"** born of a woman, would somehow redeem them and destroy the Serpent in the process, releasing them from his bondage. This is apparently all that was revealed to Adam about a future redeemer. There is nothing mentioned about a "cross" or a "new birth," all he knew was somebody was promised to come. Anyway, by God's grace Adam now had a hope to look forward to, even though he remained joined to sin and death.

Although the *Dispensation of Conscience*, began with the *Adamic Covenant*, it does not last as long as the covenant. It is replaced by another dispensation when Noah departs the ark; long before the end of the Millennium. Here is an important lesson: even though a covenant usually introduces a particular dispensation, the covenant and dispensation *do not have to end together*. A covenant can still be in effect long after its original dispensation has been replaced. Unconditional covenants can overlap each other or be in effect simultaneously, but by strict definition dispensations can not. This should become clearer as we go along.

The *Dispensation of Conscience* is so named because during this period man had nothing to guide him but his conscience. God did not give any specific commands to anyone during this dispensation. There were no "thou shalts" or "thou shalt nots;" God just left man to his own heart to guide him. Needless to say, man utterly failed in following his conscience. For the most part he hardened it and became extremely wicked. This wickedness was the cause of the flood (Gen. 6).

Some may ask here, "How could God hold them accountable for being wicked when He gave them no specific laws to keep?" The answer is man has an unwritten law written in his heart or conscience (Rom. 2:14-15). Though this law is vague compared to a written or verbal law, it will still convict a person of guilt when he contemplates evil. For instance, when Cain slew his brother Abel, he did not break any written law against murder because none was yet given, but he did break the law God had written in his heart and was therefore guilty. Like his father, Cain had a knowledge of good and evil, and he willingly chose evil. Every accountable person even today, no matter where he is, knows murder, adultery, stealing, and the like are wrong whether he has heard of the word of God or not. These laws are embedded into every man's conscience, but the conscience imparts no power to keep man from breaking it.

Man's responsibility in the *Dispensation of Conscience* (and to those in every other dispensation who have had no contact with the Scriptures) was to simply follow his conscience. If one listens carefully to his conscience, it will convict him of sin and lead him to God for salvation (Cornelius, for example, Acts 10). But if he doesn't listen to it and hardens it, all he has to look forward to is judgment. Since the people from Adam to Noah ignored their conscience and followed wickedness, God was forced to bring judgment—the flood. Man fails again.

The Noahic Covenant and
The Dispensation of Human Government

When Noah left the ark after the flood, God made His third covenant with man; the *Noahic Covenant* (Gen. 8:20-9:17). Like the previous this covenant is also unconditional and lasts until the renovation of the earth by fire (2 Pet. 3:10). In many ways God is starting over with man. Having destroyed everyone except Noah and his family because of extreme wickedness, God sought to replenish the earth through Noah because Noah found grace in His eyes (Gen. 6:8). Like the others before, this covenant contains promises TO man and responsibilities required OF man. The promises were:

- God would not curse the ground anymore or smite every living thing (Gen. 8:20).
- He would not flood the earth again and destroy it (Gen. 9:11).
- The seasons and day and night will not cease (Gen. 8:22).
- He would set the sign of a (rain)bow in the clouds as a token of His covenant (Gen. 9:12).

These promises are valid and continue regardless of man's conduct, but God also had some requirements for man to follow:

- He was to again multiply and replenish the earth (Gen. 9:1,7).
- They were not to eat blood from any source (Gen. 9:4).
- They were to exercise capital punishment upon man and beast (Gen. 9:5).

God also made two other statements related to this covenant:

- Animals would fear and dread man (Gen. 9:2).
- Animals were now available for food (Gen. 9:3).

Through the great object lesson of the flood, God showed humanity His hatred of sin. Though man often takes sin lightly, God proved

He does not and will always ultimately punish iniquity. Also seen in this is God's long-suffering nature. The Lord will sometimes delay punishment to allow space for repentance. This is clear from the grace found in the above promises to Noah. God knows that because of the fall of Adam, every man is born inherently wicked. Because of this He will not smite the earth again in the same manner since He has made His will clearly known about sin with the flood. In the future He will destroy the Antichrist and all his followers at the second advent, but he will not destroy the earth itself until his great scheme of things concerning it is over, and then only with *fire*.

Much of man's obligations under this covenant are still in effect today and will continue until the elements melt with fervent heat (2 Pet. 3:10). The command against the eating of blood is also found in the New Testament (Acts 15:29) and capital punishment is still God's will even if many today ignore it (Rom. 13:4). Remember, the subject of capital punishment was first brought up by God. There is no record it was ever practiced before God made the command to Noah. It is solely His idea and shows the sanctity of human life and the consequences of taking it with malice. Under the law God gave more details concerning its implementation.

Rebellion at Babel

The primary responsibility of man in the *Noahic Covenant* was to **"be fruitful and multiply and REPLENISH THE EARTH,"** but in this also he miserably failed. The earth's population did rapidly increase after the flood, but all the people stayed near an area later known as *Babel.* God wanted man to scatter and repopulate the whole earth, not remain in one area. The failure of man to do this brought upon him another judgment.

The descendants of Noah directly rebelled against the command to scatter and sought to stay united around a great city and tower in the plain of Shinar. In a few short years they also abandoned God in all their thoughts like those before the flood, and their greatest fear was not to displease God, but that they would be scattered. They thought safety was in numbers. It appears they built the city, with its tower, to act as a political, cultural, and religious center for them to gather around and become as a group, *self-reliant*. They thought they did not need any God and could "make the world a better place to live in" by themselves. God looked down and saw how they were one in language and purpose (what man says he strives for today), and how they were on the verge of making their imaginations real (likely with autos, airplanes, spacecraft, computers, or similar), and He decided to scatter them Himself.

God was not yet ready for man to advance in knowledge and technology as much as the people of Babel were capable of, so He did the simplest thing; He confounded their language. There were some vital lessons God wanted man to learn about himself and his Creator over the coming centuries before He would allow them to advance that far. Clearly, God is a *segregator*. The world at that time was determined to stay united and integrated, but God had other plans. The confounding of their language (certainly Hebrew) and resulting scattering was also a punishment for their disobedience. The different tongues made the respective groups unfamiliar with each other, and each language group became primarily occupied with getting and keeping territory, goods, and wealth from the other, now strange, groups. Building a one world empire was in the meanwhile forgotten. Most of the wars, famines, and other forms of suffering found throughout history are a direct result of the rebellion of the world at Babel.

The *Dispensation of Human Government,* which ran from Noah to Abraham, made man responsible for governing himself when he did wrong. God gave him very basic principles (listed above) to guide him in this, and man was required to keep them. Since man would not listen to his conscience and let it lead him to God, God made mankind as a whole responsible for punishing the sins of individuals and keeping iniquity in check. Of course, in this also man failed, but now he cannot come to God and say he wasn't given a chance to try! Instead of forming a government that was consistent with God and His commands, man developed one that was directly against him. As the one world, global, universal, United Nations, common market, Babel of today, the Babel of 4300 years ago was more concerned about unity and progress than about their sins and God.

Before we move on there is another covenant-like setup found in this dispensation between God and Noah's three sons (Gen. 9:20-29). After Noah heard the details of the above covenant, he planted a vineyard and became drunk from the wine it produced. While he was in this drunken state his son, Ham, came in unto him and saw his **"nakedness."** In other words Ham *sodomized* his father (Gen. 9:24; Lev. 18:6). When Noah recovered from his wine and realized what Ham had **"done unto him,"** he cursed Ham's seed in the person of his son Canaan. He didn't curse Ham himself because God had previously blessed him (Gen. 9:1). Noah then continues to make a series of prophetic statements that may have been somewhat vague to his three sons (the fathers of the three races), but events that have occurred down through history since make them clearer to us.

- Canaan (Ham's seed) is cursed to be a servant of his brethren (Shem and Japeth). Since the descendants of Ham moved south toward Africa, making him the father of the black race, this curse begins to fall into place. For millennia members of the black race have been slaves to other men.
- Shem on the other hand is blessed. Noah said **"blessed be the Lord God of Shem,"** and we learn later Shem is an ancestor of Abraham and the Lord Jesus Christ. God blessed the world with a Savior through Shem.
- Japeth also is blessed, and he was to be enlarged and dwell in the former dwelling places (tents) of Shem. If at no other time, this has come to pass in the last 500 years. Thousands of Japethites (Europeans) crossed the Atlantic into North and South America, into dwelling places of Shemites.

These blessings and curse have come to pass in every detail. Shem is the religious race (every major religion came from him); Japeth is the worldly, materialistic race; and Canaan is their servant. Of course, there are many individual exceptions to this, but throughout history they have racially proven to be consistent.

The Abrahamic Covenant
and The Dispensation of Promise

Nine generations after Shem, Abraham was born. Abraham was about 75 years old and living in Ur of the Chaldees when God one day spoke to him. God, through His amazing grace, wanted to make another covenant with man and chose Abraham as His partner. The covenant He made with him was again unconditional and contained many promises (Gen 12:1-3). The only hint of a condition appears to be that Abraham had to forsake his home and family and go to a land God would show him. When Abraham obeyed and entered the land the promises became fixed. God promised to:

- Make Abraham a great nation (vs. 2). This promise has been fulfilled both physically and spiritually. Physically through Isaac and Ishmael, spiritually through all those who have Abraham's faith (Gal. 3:7).
- To bless him (vs. 2), and He did this also both physically (13:14-18) and spiritually (15:6).
- To make his name great (vs. 2). Still today the name of Abraham is known and respected by millions.
- Make him a blessing to others (vs. 2). Abraham blessed people in his own time and blessed humanity by his seed Jesus Christ.
- To bless those who bless him (vs. 3).
- And curse those who curse him (vs. 3). God has not only blessed those who blessed Abraham, but He also blessed those who blessed the nation that sprang from his loins, Israel. On the other hand, those who cursed Israel (Babylon, Assyria, Rome, Germany, etc.) must suffer. Some have suffered already, but these promises will not be completely fulfilled until the future.
- Bless all the families of the earth in him (vs. 3). The fulfillment of this is Christ himself, who blesses all those who believe on Him with salvation and who will also physically bless all who are in the millennium.

Though this covenant is unconditional it does not apply universally to everyone. Doctrinally, it only applies to the Hebrew race through Isaac and Jacob (Israel). Gentiles can only get in on it by receiving Abraham's promised Seed—Jesus Christ. Those who refuse to receive Him, Jew or Gentile, will be judged by Him.

Like the *Noahic Covenant* this covenant also has a sign, and it is *circumcision* (Gen. 17:9-14). Circumcision is a token of the promises God has made to Abraham and his seed, and anyone who refused or neglected to accept it was cut off from his people and the promises (excommunication). Circumcision was the only obligation Abraham and his people had under this covenant. If they performed it by faith, they had full access to all the promises. God again reconfirmed this covenant in Genenis chapter 15 after Abraham **"believed in the Lord..."** and asked for more details. After Abraham offered five offerings as God commanded, the Lord again affirmed the covenant and revealed how Abraham's seed would be a stranger in a land (Egypt) and afflicted for 400 years. God also revealed the boundaries of the land given to Abraham. Moreover, God promised all of this to Abraham while Abraham was *asleep!* This proves the covenant is unconditional. God reconfirmed the covenant again after Abraham passed his severe but revealing test of offering Isaac (Gen. 22:15-18).

Another significant thing about this covenant is it apparently has no ending. It goes beyond the Millennium and renovation of the earth and even past the New Heaven and New Earth. Therefore, the nation of Israel, governed by its Messiah and King, will still be in existence at the gate of eternity.

The dispensation that began with this covenant is called the *Dispensation of Promise* for obvious reasons. For the first time God has made promises to one group of people at the exclusion of all others. From the time of Abraham on in the Old Testament, the only way someone other than an Israelite could partake of the promises was to become an Israelite himself (Ruth, for example [Ruth 1:16]). Again, the only way now is to receive Jesus Christ. By some this dispensation is called the *Dispensation of the Family* because everything God had to say to man He said to this one family. The promises He made to Abraham He reconfirmed to his son Isaac, his grand-son Jacob, and then to Jacob's sons, the heads of the twelve tribes of Israel. The manner of behavior God expected in this dispensation is much like the previous except that He told Abraham to go to a certain land and stay there (Canaan).

Abraham obeyed in going to the land, but when a famine came and times got hard he fled into Egypt for food. He could not yet trust God enough to stay. This again shows the weakness and failure of man to live up to God's requirements. In every dispensation man in some way fails to keep God's word and consequently brings judgment upon himself.

Moreover, the character of the descendants of Abraham degenerated from that of Abraham. Even though Abraham was afraid and lied in Egypt about Sarah, Isaac seemed to lie more easily (Gen. 26:7). Jacob (meaning Deceiver or Supplanter) was even more blatant in sin. He lied, deceived, tricked, and schemed it appears without a second thought (Gen. 27:6-29). Likewise, his sons (with the exception of Joseph) were even more mixed up in vice and evil. From adultery with handmaids and harlots to murder and kidnapping (Gen. 34:25, 37:23-36, 38:12-18), they all seemed to think lightly of sin. The actions of everyone concerned, from Abraham on down, and the degeneration of the character of the family in each succeeding generation caused God to send Abraham's seed into Egypt and later into bondage. It was 430 years from the call of Abraham to the exodus from Egypt, the length of this dispensation.

The Mosaic Covenant
and The Dispensation of the Law

By the time Moses was born, the 75 people that went with Jacob into Egypt had grown into millions. The new king that **"knew not Joseph"** put them into heavy bondage and eventually the Israelites began to cry upon the Lord for deliverance. God heard their cry and sent them a deliverer from among their own—Moses. Since the self-governing of man in the dispensations of Conscience and Promise failed, God established a highly comprehensive and detailed dispensation where He could rule man Himself from a central place of worship.

After revealing Himself to Moses in the wilderness, God sent Moses back into Egypt to free his brethren from their slavery. With great signs and wonders He performed through Moses, God forced Israel's release and brought the people across the Red Sea to make a nation out of them as He promised to Abraham. On their way to the promised land (Canaan), God established His covenant with them at Mt. Sinai, and this time the covenant is completely conditional. That is, for God to continue to do His part, the Israelites had to continue to do theirs. The bulk of this covenant is called **"the law,"** a detailed list of rules and regulations concerning nearly every aspect of life. No longer were they to be guided only by their conscience or the opinions of other men, God had given them very specific WRITTEN commands which were easily understood and could be consulted at any time.

In Exodus 19:5-6 God, through Moses, lays the covenant before the people and tells them what He will do for them **"if"** they obey His voice. The people of one accord reply **"All that the Lord has spoken we will do"** (Ex. 19:8) and the covenant is sealed. In the next chapter God gives them the "Ten Commandments," and in much of the rest of Exodus, nearly all of Leviticus, and a good portion of Numbers and Deuteronomy, He reveals more requirements. This covenant can be broken into three parts:

- The *Moral Law* (Ex. 20: 1-26, the Ten Commandments, etc.).
- The *Civil (or Judicial) Law* (Ex. 21:1-24:18). This was the precepts of the judicial system for the punishment of crimes and settlement of disputes.
- The *Ceremonial Law* (Ex. 25:1-40:38, etc.). This was in essence their religious system and included all the details of sacrifice and worship (the tabernacle, priesthood, offerings, etc.).

This covenant also has a sign: the Sabbath day—the seventh day of the week (Saturday [Ex. 31:13-17]).

Here, we must remind the reader that this covenant was only between *God and the Israelites.* No part of it applied to any Gentile then and neither does it now. The moral law of God found in the Ten Commandments is a reflection of God's nature and is profitable for anyone in any dispensation, but *doctrinally* as given in Exodus and Deuteronomy they are binding only on the Jews. All of the commandments, excluding the fifth (the sabbath), can be found in some form in the New Testament, thus making their message apply also to born again Christians, but as they are found in the *Mosaic Covenant,* they apply ONLY to Israel.

As we have said much of the Scripture wresting that goes on today is a result of people not properly dividing the Scriptures and forcing doctrines from one dispensational arrangement into another. The Sabbath, for instance, is one that is today heavily abused. God clearly states in Ex. 31:13-17 that the Sabbath is to and for the children of Israel alone and binding on no one else. Some think since it is found in the Ten Commandments it is an "eternal" law to everyone, but as mentioned above, no one else was ever commanded to keep it. In fact a born again Christian is not commanded to set apart any particular day for worship, not even the Lord's day (Sunday). He is free to meet on any day he esteems best (Rom. 14:5). Most believers usually meet on the Lord's day, however, by following the examples found in the New Testament (Acts 20:7, etc.). Again, when one tries to place a doctrine peculiar to one dispensation into another he will always end up with heresy.

The *Dispensation of the Law* lasted from the exodus out of Egypt until the cross (around 1500 years), and God kept his part of the covenant despite many failures of the Israelites to keep theirs. Just a short period of time after they promised to obey it, the Jews rebelled against the Lord, but God graciously gave them many more chances to obey. When they rebelled against Moses over the bitter water, God made the water sweet (Ex. 15:25). When they murmured about the lack of food, God gave them manna for 40 years (Ex. 16). When they became idolaters and worshipped the golden calf, clearly breaking the covenant, God again had grace and mercy on them though He had a mind to do otherwise (Ex. 32).

Over the years God was very long-suffering with Israel and overlooked many of their transgressions. When Moses died God was gracious and gave them another leader, Joshua. When he died God gave them judges to lead them. When they sought to be like the heathen and wanted a king, God warned them against it but nevertheless gave them Saul. After Saul came a man after His own heart, David. After David, God gave them His wisdom through Solomon, and on and on. God gave His people every advantage and opportunity to love obey and serve Him as He desired, but the Jews were a stiff-necked and rebellious people. With a pitiful few short periods of semi-obedience and loyalty to their credit, the Jews were usually characterized by *rebellion, immorality, and idolatry.*

Though God was long-suffering with Israel, He would not put up with their rebellion forever, and after almost 1000 years His patience ran out. In the meantime He sent numerous prophets (Isaiah, Jeremiah, Ezekiel, etc.) to warn them of what He was about to do if they didn't repent, but for the most part they either ignored them or persecuted them. God faithfully protected Israel from her enemies for centuries, but around 606 BC, because of their failure to return to Him, He let their enemies have them. The Babylonians destroyed Jerusalem and carried the people into Babylon to again be slaves. Only after 70 years, after a new generation came along, did God allow them to return to Jerusalem and rebuild it under Ezra and Nehemiah. Though they rebuilt it with the purest of intentions, they again, over the next four centuries, degenerated and became so filled with unbelief, self-righteousness, and hatred that they *did not even recognize their own promised Messiah* when He walked among them (Jn. 1:10-11)! More than that they mercilessly persecuted and then crucified Him! So much for the humanistic notions there is "a spark of divinity in every man" or "man is basically good."

God has up to this point set up five different doctrinal arrangements with man, five different methods of testing and dealing with him, and man has *miserably failed* in every one!

The Davidic Covenant
and The Dispensation of Grace

This covenant and dispensational arrangement is different from the others because the covenant is given nearly 1000 years before it and its accompanying dispensation go into effect. Instead of starting when it was first mentioned, this covenant is not fully in effect until David's seed comes along (Jesus Christ).

Once when Israel was at peace and David was at rest from his enemies, David wanted to do something for God and proposed building Him a permanent house (temple) to dwell in. Through Nathan the prophet God told David He did not yet want a house, but appreciated the thought (1 Ki. 8:18), and He then told David He was going to make a house out of HIM.

God made three promises to David in this unconditional covenant found in 2 Sam. 7:4-17:

- That his house (posterity) would never cease (vs. 12-13).
- That his throne will never be completely destroyed and continue forever (vs. 13, 16).
- That his earthly kingdom will also continue forever through his promised seed (vs. 13, 16).

In some respects this covenant could be speaking of Solomon as the seed, but Solomon's reign ended in apostasy (1 Kings 11), thus another seed of David must be the ultimate fulfillment—the *Lord Jesus Christ*. Christ is the only person who can possibly fulfill it. He is the seed of *Adam, Shem, Abraham, Isaac, Jacob, Judah,* and *David,* and he is the only person in history who fulfills the more than sixty other prophesies God had given concerning the **"seed."** Before Christ was born the angel Gabriel told Mary the son to be born of her was to be the **"son of the highest"** (God), the **"son of David"** (man), and He would reign on David's throne forever (Luke 1:30-33). This covenant, like the *Abrahamic Covenant* continues to the gate of eternity.

Since the fulfillment of this covenant is Jesus Christ, and God is going to keep all of His promises to David in Christ, the covenant did not come into effect until Christ was born. That no seed of David has reigned in Jerusalem since the Babylonian captivity has nothing to do with the fulfillment of this covenant. It is not until after Israel's full chastisement for rejecting Christ is completed (Tribulation) that Christ comes as a King to reign on David's throne (Millennium).

Christ came the first time as a *Servant and sacrificial Lamb;* the second time He will come as a *Warrior and King.*

The dispensation ushered in by the *Davidic Covenant* is our present *Dispensation of Grace.* Again, that this dispensation is named grace does not mean that God's grace cannot be found in the other dispensations, only that it is more prevalent and visible in this one. God often had mercy and grace on many in the past (Adam, Noah, Abraham, David, etc.), but now He freely offers His saving grace to everyone through the shed blood of the Lord Jesus Christ.

Technically, this dispensation does not begin with Christ's birth but with his death and resurrection. It extends from the cross to the calling up of all believers, dead or alive, at the rapture. (1 Thes. 4:13-18). In some ways this is a parenthetical dispensation because it is in the form of a mystery and sandwiched between the two Jewish dispensations of Law and the Millennium.

The subject of this dispensation is a group called **"the church"** or **"the body of Christ."** The Church is the mystery referred to in Eph. 3:3-9 and is so named because God had not revealed in the Old Testament that He was going to form such an organism, especially from both Jews and Gentiles. The New Testament tells us God's purpose in the Church is to gather a **"people for His name"** from all humanity, Jew and Gentile, in Jesus Christ to (among other things) become Christ's bride. **"Whosoever will"** can become a member of this living organism by simply repenting and by faith receiving the risen Jesus Christ into his heart. No works are required to obtain or keep this eternal salvation; all one must have is Jesus Christ in him. Christ has promised to freely come into and save all who will admit they are sinners, abandon all other means of salvation, and trust Him alone as Savior.

In this dispensation God is no longer dealing with man primarily as nations but as *individuals.* Every individual can have a personal relationship with God through the Lord Jesus Christ and he does not have to go through any priest or religious system to receive atonement for his sins. Israel, as a nation, has been placed on a "back burner" because of their blindness, but individual Jews can be saved just the same as Gentiles until this dispensation ends. The **"Church of God"** is a distinct body from both Jews and Gentiles and has many blessings these two groups don't enjoy. God has poured many extremely rich blessings upon the saved of this dispensation that He has not given to those of any other. Even those saved in future dispensations do not have many of the precious treasures the Body of Christ has now. For example:

- The *new birth* (regeneration [Tit. 3:5, etc.]). There is no clear, biblical proof that the new birth is valid in any other dispensation (More on this later).
- A *completed atonement* (described under the salvation doctrines propitiation and redemption [Heb. 9:12; 1 Jn. 2:2]). Until Christ's death salvation was "on credit."
- *Eternal and everlasting life* that the believer cannot loose (described under the salvation doctrines justification, adoption, reconciliation, imputation, etc. [John 3:16, 5:24; etc.])
- *Salvation by faith alone,* no works at all required to obtain or keep it (Eph 2:8-9; etc.).
- The *indwelling Holy Spirit* who comforts, empowers, and seals believers (Eph. 4:30).
- A *position in Christ's Body* and Bride (Eph. 5:30-32).
- The *promise of a supernatural body* like Christ's resurrection body (Phil. 3:21).
- A *future mansion* in the New Jerusalem (John 14:1-3).

Clearly, born again Christians, by no value of their own, have been given more blessings and promises than any other group of saved people, all by the good pleasure and pure grace of God. Why God selected this group to shower these amazing privileges on is fully known only by Him, but how much more should we who are saved and partake of them obey God's wishes with love and thanksgiving?

The obligation of believers during this dispensation is simple and direct. Each believer is to:

- *Evangelize* by preaching the gospel of the grace of God to every creature (Matt. 28:19-20; Mark 16:15).
- Be *filled with the Holy Spirit* and let Him direct his every thought and action (Gal. 5:16; Eph.5:18).

- *Present himself as a living sacrifice* for God's service and separate himself from the world (Rom. 12:1-2).

Whether the believer obeys or disobeys these duties has nothing to do with his salvation, but disobedience will cost him rewards and crowns at the Judgment Seat of Christ where every believer will give account of himself to God (Rom. 14:10).

Even with the multitude of great blessings and privileges God has showered upon believers in Christ, this dispensation still ends in failure. Their failure was hinted at by Christ before the cross. He said when He returned the times would then be like the days of Noah thousands of years earlier (Matt. 24:37-39), characterized by unrestrained rebellion, wickedness, and apostasy. With all God has given believers in this present dispensation, they have again willingly refused to consistently do as He commanded.

Soon Christ will return and secretly take away all the Christians to Heaven and judgment and let the world continue, then even faster, toward its destiny of destruction.

The Tribulation Period

Sometime after the rapture, possibly immediately or maybe years later, the *Tribulation Period* will began. In Jer. 30:6 this period is called **"the time of Jacob's trouble"** because God is going to judge Israel as a nation by allowing Satan to **"trouble"** them (through the Antichrist) for rejecting Jesus Christ as their Messiah. Though Satan will have his own reasons for punishing the Jews, God will allow him to do it because they said concerning Christ **"crucify him, crucify him"** (John 19:6) and **"his blood be on us and on our CHILDREN"** (Matt. 27:25). God simply gives them their request. This is the time period Christ was referring to when He said, **"...for then shall be great tribulation, such as was not since the beginning of the world to this time, no, nor ever shall be"** (Matt. 24:21). It will be disaster and sorrow on such a scale that the strongest men will hide in caves and beg for death (Rev. 6:15-16).

When Christ said, **"I am come in my father's name, and ye receive me not, if another will come in his own name him ye will receive"** (John 5:44), He was speaking of the coming Antichrist (also called **"the Beast," "the man of sin,"** the **"abomination of desolation,"** etc.). This evil character is second only to Christ as to the amount of information the Bible gives him. Daniel tells us he will make a covenant with Israel (Dan. 9:27) for **"seven weeks"** (years) and then break it in the middle (at 42 months). Many Jews will think him to be their Messiah until he breaks the covenant and demands to be worshipped as the God of Heaven (2 Thes. 2:4). When the Jews refuse, the Beast (now Satan incarnate) will persecute them with a fierce vengeance. He will slaughter millions of them (and also Gentiles who refuse to worship his image or take his mark—666, Rev. 13), but 144,000 will be sealed by God and protected from harm.

Finally, after no more than seven years from the signing of the covenant, Jesus Christ will return and destroy the Beast and his armies at Armageddon. The few Jews that are left will then **"look upon him whom they pierced"** and receive Christ as their true Messiah and King. At that moment God will save them as a nation (Rom. 11:26). They will, after 20 centuries, have finally accepted Christ for WHO He really is—**"God manifest in the flesh."** Though the Tribulation will severely punish them, almost to extinction, God was forced to allow it to get them to receive the truth. Being "stiff-necked" (Acts 7:51) they would not accept it under any other means. Once they repent and receive Jesus Christ, they are then ready to receive the kingdom promised to their fathers Abraham and David.

Dispensationally, the Tribulation period is basically the *Dispensation of the Law* with a few added features. Since the Church will have left in the rapture, the parenthetical *Dispensation of Grace* will be gone along with the doctrines unique to it. Thus the nation of Israel will again be the main object of God's concern. There will be a temple in the *Tribulation,* sacrifices will be offered, and salvation will again have a Jewish ring to it. More on this in the following chapters.

The Palestinian Covenant, The New Covenant, and The Messianic Dispensation

1400 years before Christ, at the end of their 40 years of wandering in the wilderness, God made another covenant with Israel besides the one He made at Mt. Sinai. Called the *Palestinian Covenant* because they were about to enter the land of Palestine, the covenant contains a promise of what God will do for them when they repent of their sins and return to Him after a period of rebellion. God promised after He dispersed them among the nations as punishment for future disobedience (ultimately the rejection of Christ), He would regather and return them to their land after they repent. This covenant is closely linked with the *Mosaic Covenant,* and some say the two are joined together at the beginning of the Millennium. It is found in Deut. 30:1-10 and its specific elements are:

- Israel's dispersion for disobedience (vs. 1). Though Israel is a nation today, more Jews live in New York City than in the land of Palestine. The bulk of the Jews on earth are still scattered and those in Israel do not possess all the land promised to them.
- Their (foreknown) repentance while dispersed (vs. 2). This is during the Tribulation.
- The return of the Lord (vs. 3). Christ will personally regather them after the Tribulation.
- The restoration of all their land (vs. 5). Christ will give them the entire land grant promised to Abraham.
- Their national conversion (vs. 6). All Israel will be saved (nationally) in a day (Rom. 11:26).
- The judgment of their enemies and oppressors (vs. 7). The judgment of the nations (Matt. 25).
- Their national blessing and prosperity (vs. 9).

This covenant comes into effect at the end of the Tribulation period when the remaining Jews see the return of the Lord Jesus Christ and receive Him as their Messiah. They will nationally repent and mourn for their sin of rejecting Him and admit before all their acceptance of Him as King. God will then, in Christ, forgive them and bless them as He desired to bless them from their beginning. He will give them all the land promised to their fathers and reign over them Himself from Jerusalem. Christ will judge their enemies at the Judgment of Nations (Matt. 25:31-46) and place the other nations under them in privilege and importance. Israel will be the premier nation on earth, and that purely by the promise and good pleasure of God. This covenant lasts, at least, until the end of the Millennium.

The *New Covenant* is called **"new"** because unlike the previous covenants it has not yet been made. It was promised in Jer. 31:31-37 and confirmed again in Heb. 8:7-13, but it has not yet been officially given to the nation of Israel. Again, after the Jews repent and receive Christ as their Messiah, God will formally establish this unconditional covenant with them. This is the **"new testament"** Jesus was referring to in Matt. 26:28 when He said, **"for this is my blood of the new testament, which is shed for many for the remission of sins."** Thus this covenant is based on the shed blood and atoning death of Jesus Christ.

Many today insist this New Covenant doctrinally applies to the present "church age," but this is another wresting of Scripture. By letting the Scriptures speak for themselves one can easily see that the New Covenant only applies doctrinally to **"the house of Israel"** and **"the house of Judah"** (Jer. 31:31, Heb. 8:8). It has nothing to do with the born again believer or the present Dispensation of Grace. The main thrust of this **"new testament"** is not the Church Age, but a future covenant with Israel based on the atoning death of the Jewish **"testator,"** Jesus Christ. Of course, the salvation Christ bought with His blood is available to all today, Jew or Gentile, but as found in Jeremiah and Hebrews the New Covenant will apply only to Israel. The specifics of this covenant are (as found in Jeremiah 31):

- God will put His laws in each individual's heart (vs. 33).
- God will again be their God and Israel His people (vs. 33).
- There will no longer be any preaching or witnessing because all Jews will know the Lord (vs. 34).
- God will completely forgive them and remember their sin no more (vs. 34).

- It is as permanent as day and night, the moon and stars, the waves of the sea, and the unmeasurable vastness of the earth and heavens (vs. 35-37).

This covenant is in effect from the beginning of the Millennium through to the gate of eternity.

The *Messianic Dispensation* (the Millennium), along with the *New Covenant*, will begin when the *Palestinian Covenant* is fulfilled at the end of the *Tribulation*. This dispensation is the "golden age" and "utopia" man today dreams about. It will be characterized by *a perfect, righteous, and holy Ruler, universal righteousness, world peace, greatly reduced sickness and death, extended life span, gentleness and compatibility of wildlife, more cooperative earth for crops, perfect climate and environment, no random natural disasters, most of the curses lifted, little or no crime, and the binding of man's constant enemy, Satan.* In the Millennium man will have everything he says today he wants, but will he fare any better in this dispensation than in the others? Hardly.

There are scores of passages in the Old Testament concerning this blessed period, and in the New Testament it is called the **"kingdom of heaven"** (Matt. 3:2, 5:3). The kingdom of heaven truly was **"at hand"** when Christ began His earthly ministry, but when the Jews rejected the King it was postponed until they were willing to receive Him. The "sermon on the mount" (Matt. ch. 5-7) will essentially be the Constitution of this kingdom and lay down the rules and principles of behavior required in it. During this 1000 year period, Christ will rule with a **"rod of iron"** and compel everyone to obey these principles and His will. Those who don't will be punished (Zech. 14:16-19).

With Satan bound in the bottomless pit and no longer able to influence nations or individuals for evil (Rev. 20:2), man will not be able to blame him for their sins. God will remove every form of outside negative influence during the Millennium, thus giving man every opportunity to do right. But even in this much sought after environment man will ultimately fail. It appears that during this period the people will begin to get tired of compelled obedience and of the righteous King in Jerusalem and rebel against Christ in their heart (Jer. 17:9). At the end of the 1000 years, God will release Satan from prison and give him access to the nations one last time. Very quickly Satan will organize a revolt against Christ and form a huge army to oust Him from Jerusalem. He will likely use pride to convince man he can do a better job "governing himself" (remember the *Dispensation of Human Government?*). The entire revolt is devoured by fire from Heaven and Satan's usefulness to God is over (Rev. 20:9).

It has taken God seven dispensations to do it, but He has proved his point. The problem with man is not his *circumstances or misfortune,* neither is it his *environment or upbringing,* man's number one problem is *HIMSELF.* Man by *nature* is evil, and no matter what kind of world or environment he is placed in he will remain evil. The only remedy is God must give him a new heart (2 Cor. 5:17).

During this time those who make up the body of Christ and have gone up in the rapture will reign with Christ from Jerusalem. They may act as His ambassadors to the nations enforcing His righteousness all over the earth. Nevertheless, each born again believer's old sinful nature will be *literally and forever dead,* leaving him with no capacity for sin. He will also have a supernatural, glorified body like Christ's (Phil. 3:21). Therefore, he cannot rebel with the world against Christ, he has already went through his testing period. The Jews and Gentiles that enter into the Millennium from the Tribulation, however, will still have only their natural bodies and the same old sinful Adamic nature all sinners are born with.

The New Heavens,
The New Earth, and The New Jerusalem

After the rebellion at the end of the Millennium and the destruction of all those involved, God's series of testing periods for man will be over; the time for final judgment will have come. God will judge everyone who has not been judged before in a final, all encompassing judgment at the *Great White Throne.* Every saved person from Adam to the end of the Millennium who was not part of a group that was previously judged (like the Church), along with every person of every other age who died lost will be resurrected to stand before the Lord Jesus Christ and be judged according to their works. Those whose names are found in the **"book of life"** will be granted the privilege to enter into the *New Heaven and New Earth.* Those whose are not found in the book will be cast into the **"lake of fire,"** there to spend eternity in torment (Rev. 20).

Many today claim there will be no saved people from any dispensation before the White Throne for judgment, but what about those saved in the *Tribulation and Millennium?* There is no other judgment to cover these people. We agree no saved person from the present *Dispensation of Grace* will be judged there because the **"Judgment Seat of Christ"** will cover them, but those saved in other dispensations must be judged at some time (Heb. 9:27), and this is the only judgment left. These people will have their names recorded in the book of life when they are saved; the *Great White Throne Judgment* will simply reveal their salvation, and their works, to all.

While the above judgment is in progress, God will be forming the *New Heaven and the New Earth.* He will do this by renovating the old heaven and earth with fire, melting the elements and purging them from the contamination of sinful man and preparing them for future habitation. The White Throne Judgment apparently occurs in the void of space.

After the judgment and renovation God will be ready to establish His final dispensational arrangement. Calling this arrangement a dispensation may not be entirely accurate because it has no clear ending. It appears to join with eternity. Furthermore, three covenants will still be in effect at this time, the *Abrahamic, Davidic, and New Covenants;* therefore, the nation of Israel will still be in existence (Isa. 66:22).

Including Israel there will be three distinct groups of people in this final arrangement. Israel will be made up of saved Jews from every dispensation except the *Dispensation of Grace;* the second group will be saved Gentiles from every dispensation except Grace; and the third group will be all those saved, Jew and Gentile, in the *Dispensation of Grace — the Bride of Christ.* The Bride of Christ is a fixed number that cannot increase or decrease after the rapture, but the other two groups can increase through childbirth.

Since there will be no more death (Rev. 21:4), the kingdom will increase and rapidly fill the earth and then spread throughout the heavens. Isaiah 9:7 says, **"of the increase of his government there**

shall be no end," thus Christ's kingdom may expand from earth to the other planets, then to the stars and beyond towards infinity. After 7000 years of dealing with man, God has redeemed those who obeyed him and put them in a suitable condition to populate the universe. Out of billions and billions of people who have lived on earth, God has saved a relatively small remnant and these now love Him in return. With them God may begin to populate the entire universe.

The Bride of Christ will dwell in *New Jerusalem,* a city prepared by Christ for her habitation that contains "many mansions." The city will descend from Heaven to earth and among other things contain the throne of God and the **"tree of life"** (Rev. 21). At this point God will have in some respects made a complete circle in His dealings with man. The Bible begins with man in a garden with the **"tree of life,"** and after more than 7000 years of revealing many things to him, God has him again in a garden like setting with a tree that brings life.

Although there are other more minor divisions in the Bible one could mention, the eight major divisions we have outlined above are the ones most essential for understanding the Scriptures. If a believer will spend a little time in study and by noting these divisions keep the different issues separate and the alike together, he will be well on his way to understanding God's program for man and all creation as He has revealed it. Things that are different are not the same, and in the Bible *the difference is often in the dispensations.*

The Great Lesson

Of the many things God has showed man through the dispensations, the lesson that should stand out above the others is that man is *a hopeless rebel, utter failure, and without hope without God.* He is simply *not capable* of living up to God's righteous standard no matter how "enlightened" and able he may think he is.

Place him in a beautiful garden with everything he needs, including fellowship with God, a beautiful and compatible wife, the earth under his dominion, access to the Tree of Life, etc., and man will *forsake it all* and choose death. Leave him alone with his conscience to guide him and man will become so *exceedingly wicked* that he must be removed from the earth with a flood. Give him great and sure promises and man will flee them and *speak lies in unbelieving fear*. Make of him a chosen nation for God to speak through and dwell among, with His holy Law and priesthood, and man will abandon his God and *worship dumb idols*. Give him an eternal redemption from sin and hell, everlasting life, an indwelling Holy Spirit, the promise of a new body, a home in New Jerusalem, and birth him into God's own family making him His son, and man will repay his Savior with *rebellion, worldliness, and indifference*. Give him a perfect, uncursed earth, a cooperative environment, no Satan to tempt him, extended lifespan, and Jesus Christ himself to reign over him, and man will *revolt and try to force Christ from His throne*. All is clear. Man is a wicked, vile, evil, selfish, and vain creature, and apart from God he is utterly hopeless and bound for hell. The surest proof of this is God is near the last millennium of his dealings with man (now 6000 years along), and man collectively has *not learned this ONE lesson yet!*

Chapter II
Salvation In The Old Testament

From our brief overview of the major divisions of the Bible, it should be clear to the reader that God does not always work exactly the same way in every dispensation. What God required of Adam (don't eat of the tree), He did not require of Moses; what He required of Noah (ark), He did not require of David. Likewise what He required of Moses and David (keep the Law), He does not require of us today. God is the same God, but He simply *does not work with man the same way in every dispensation.* Therefore, every Christian MUST know where the divisions between the dispensations are and what God requires of man in each of them to make reasonable sense of the Bible. Again, this is imperative to see God's overall program for man as He has revealed it.

In this chapter and the following, we are going to look at the covenants and dispensations from the standpoint of *personal, individual salvation.* This is a touchy topic, but our only concern is what the Bible says about the matter. Now, we realize every Bible preacher, teacher, minister, "scholar," etc. who attempts to teach something from the Bible says he is only interested in what the Bible says; therefore, the reader must determine the truth himself through *prayer and study.* Don't blindly follow the opinions of men no matter how "godly," "devoted," and "fundamental" they may appear; follow only the BOOK (*AV 1611*). When anyone (including your author) does not strictly go by the Bible, abandon him, at least in the area of error. The Bible is the Christian's absolute, final authority for ALL matters and is subject to no individual, group, church, or school.

Before we go any farther, let us clear the air and list three "historic, fundamental positions" we take issue with concerning salvation:

- That the means of receiving salvation is *exactly* the same in every dispensation.
- That *every person* ever saved was **"born again"** and a "son of God."

- That no saved person in any age can in any way *lose his salvation.*

These three positions are considered "undeniable" among many today, but again, **"what saith the Scriptures"**?

First of all, before you jump to conclusions, let us state as clearly as we can that we fully believe every person saved in this present Church Age is saved by *grace through faith apart from any works.* We insist he is *born again, a son of God, and has eternal, everlasting life abiding in him which he cannot lose.* We further believe in all the baptistic "fundamentals of the faith," and more than that we believe the book these fundamentals were extracted from — the *Authorized King James Version of 1611.* Our only real difference with some of the brethren is we don't believe all these Baptist fundamentals apply to *everyone in every dispensation.* We contend the new birth, eternal security, the Body of Christ, permanently indwelling Holy Spirit, and all other doctrines unique to the Church Age were not available until *after* the crucifixion, were not revealed until the New Testament was well under way, and were not clearly defined until the epistles of Paul. We further contend these Church Age doctrines have no application to any Old Testament saint, no matter how notable (Abraham, Moses, David, etc..), or to someone in the Tribulation.

Nowhere in the Old Testament can one find the Holy Spirit regenerating anyone, sealing anyone unto the **"day of redemption,"** placing someone **"in Christ,"** or applying a half dozen other New Testament doctrines, but that doesn't stop people from teaching these doctrines are there. They do it by taking present Baptist (or any other) Church Age doctrines and forcing them to apply to all ages. This is nearly as bad as those who try to force doctrines unique to the Law (the Sabbath, abstaining from certain meats, etc.) on believers today. The only difference is the Baptist doctrines cannot be practiced in the past because they were unknown then, but past doctrines can be practiced now. In future dispensations, though, those who try to force presently sound Baptist doctrine to apply there will be heretics just like the Sabbath-keepers and pork-abstainers are today. As someone has said, "Nearly every bad thing is a good thing twisted," thus even the precious new birth can be detrimental if it is taught as doctrine in the wrong age.

When one reads modern, "fundamental" literature he needs to be careful. Much of what he reads will likely be sound doctrine, but some may also be based solely on assumption, emotion, opinion, or ignorance. For example, the author has read and heard several respected ministers make statements like: "People in the Old Testament were saved by looking forward to the cross while people in the New Testament are saved by looking back to the cross...," "All Old Testament saints were saved just like we are today...," "All believers from every age are born again, possessors of eternal life, and part of the Body of Christ...," etc., and make no effort to PROVE these statements from the Bible. They make them in such a matter of fact manner that the hearer usually does not even question them. He accepts them as "universal truths" from the lips of a great "scholar" or preacher. Though these remarks may sound biblical to modern ears, that does not MAKE them biblical.

For instance, concerning Old Testament saints "looking forward to the cross," what cross? A **"cross"** is not mentioned in any context in the Bible until Matthew 10:38, and a cross is not directly connected with Jesus Christ's death until Matthew 20:19! Where does that leave *Joseph, Aaron, Gideon and the rest of the Old Testament saints?* How could they look forward to something that did not exist and God had not yet revealed? *Christ's own disciples who followed him for months didn't even understand why Christ had to die, let alone "look ahead to a cross"* (Matt. 16:22). You say, "Well, they were looking forward to redemption, then, if not a cross." Maybe so, but what did they know about redemption (Heb. 9:12)? Did they know as much about it as Paul in Romans, John in 1 John, or even YOU today? Did they know anything about someone dying on a cross for the sins of the world to purchase and provide an eternal redemption from sin? When Christ told Peter about His coming crucifixion it was such a shock to Peter that he rebuked Him! Peter didn't want to even consider his master dying on a cross, so to say he was looking forward to it absurd. We admit it is easy to apply our rich salvation doctrines and advanced revelations to those of other dispensations, so we must be extra careful when dividing the Scriptures to only apply to a dispensation the doctrines valid at that time.

One of the strongest indications that salvation is not the same in every age is that Old Testament saints did not go at death to the same place New Testament saints go to when they die. Old Testament saints went to Abraham's Bosom or **"paradise"** while New Testament saints go directly into the presence of God in Heaven (2 Cor. 5:8). This alone proves there is a difference. Christ cleared up the matter in Luke 16 concerning where dead believers at that time went with the account of the "Rich man and Lazarus." Before Christ, the Bible was not clear where believers went at death. That there was a hell for the wicked was clear, but specific details concerning where believers went were not revealed. All that is said of Abraham, for instance, is that he was **"gathered unto his people."** In Luke 16 the Lord gives advanced revelation and says Abraham was actually in a desirable and comfortable place (called **"paradise"** in Luke 23:43) across a great gulf from Hell.

Abraham and the other saints did not go into Heaven until they went up with the Lord at His ascension (Eph. 4:8), but saints who die in the Lord today go immediately into Heaven (2 Cor. 5:8). Obviously, our salvation is in significant ways different than Abraham's. In light of their many similarities, the two salvations are quite different.

In the following we are going to look at salvation in the various dispensations and examine the similarities and differences between them. We will be very careful and try not to make the mistakes of many today who read doctrines from one period into another, forcing the Bible line up with their **"private interpretation."** Remember, the Bible is not a Baptist book written only for Baptists (or others) in this present age, it is a Jewish book written to people of all ages declaring different manners and doctrines for each period.

Innocent Adam

Before the fall Adam was not in a "lost" condition, thus he didn't need to be saved from non-existent sins. But, as we mentioned before, Adam was not righteous either. Adam and Eve are the only people ever who have been in such a purely innocent state. When they were created, they didn't have any acquired knowledge of anything. Even with all their potential "brain power," they were essentially in a state of ignorance. Though Adam was created a full grown man (likely appearing around 30 years old), he knew nothing about being a full grown man. All he knew was what God had built into him as instinct. As soon as he became conscious, however, Adam began to learn things through three methods: he learned from *observation,* he learned by *attempting to do things* (experience), and he learned what God revealed to him with *WORDS.* Adam knew nothing about holiness, righteousness, purity, etc., nor about rebellion, wickedness, sin, and salvation. He was truly innocent—but also ignorant of the most essential things. All he knew about his Creator was what He revealed to him, and essentially all God revealed to him about Himself and His nature can be found in Genesis chapters 1-2 under the Edenic Covenant (see chapter 1).

Notice when instructing Adam God does not go into long speeches about the benefits of doing right and the consequences of doing wrong. He knew Adam had no experimental concept of these matters. What is "right" to someone who has never seen or experienced "wrong"? On the other hand, what is "wrong" to someone who has never consciously chosen to do "right"? God was testing Adam in Eden and gave him a free will to make a choice, but the choice, as far as Adam is concerned, is not between "right and wrong," *but between God and something else!*

Before He would let Adam stumble upon it by accident, God, in love, warned him of the deadly result of eating of the Tree of Knowledge. Since Adam had no concept of "wrong," God did not tell him it was wrong to eat of it. He told him only that it would kill him and it was His will for him NOT to eat of it. True, Adam didn't know what death was either, but he didn't have to, to make the right choice. Wasn't God's WORDS telling him He didn't want him to eat of it enough? Adam didn't have to know all the details. God's warning showed Adam He loved him, cared for him, and didn't want him to die. Furthermore, God also put the **"Tree of Life"** in the garden to give Adam a positive alternative, but neither was it "right" to eat of this tree. Again, the test was not between right and wrong or good and evil, but would man love God in return for His love and obey Him, or love *something else* more.

The Serpent also knew of Adam and Eve's moral ignorance, and he used it to further his evil purpose. As mentioned before Satan used the desire for "knowledge" to deceive Eve into eating of the forbidden tree, but Adam, who was NOT deceived and who heard the warning directly from God's mouth, decided he loved Eve more than he loved God and ate also. Though he knew his action was against God's will, Adam was willing to suffer death with Eve ("whatever that is," there was no death before the fall) rather than live with God. As a result of eating Adam, became a "sinner." He received the lusted for knowledge of good and evil, but he also became *lost, spiritually dead, headed for physical death, alienated from God, and afraid in the process.* He gained much knowledge in a few short moments, but definitely the wrong kind.

When Adam ate he did not fall from what we consider today as salvation, but he did fall from innocence to sin, from a relatively safe position into iniquity. When he was in innocence (remember, not righteousness) he was much better off than in guilt, and in this sense he fell from safety—salvation. On the other hand, if Adam had eaten of the Tree of Life instead he may have acquired *righteousness.* Though the Bible does not plainly say that he would, it is somewhat implied since he obtained an evil nature from the Tree of Knowledge. If this is true and he did eat of the Tree of Life instead of the Tree of Knowledge, he would have still obtained the knowledge they desired. Not by doing a sinful act, but by doing a righteous act. They would have knowledge similar to the way God has knowledge of good and evil. Not by committing an act of sin and realizing righteousness as the opposite, but by doing an act of righteousness and knowing sin as the opposite.

God does not have to be a sinner to know what sin is. Since He is righteous by nature, He knows sin is everything that is contrary to Him. Everything and anything contrary to God is sin. He is the absolute standard, and His infallible word is His vehicle to convey this standard to man. Adam likely would have known this too if he had loved God enough to eat of the right tree. Having only a righteous nature he would have been saved from the possibility of sinning (eternal security) because *a righteous man cannot sin!*

Nevertheless, what we want the reader to realize is Adam's "salvation" before the fall was based entirely upon *works.* If Adam neglected the work of eating from the freely offered Tree of Life (as he did), he would never have had all God wanted for him (eternal life, righteousness, etc.). If he refused to eat of the forbidden Tree of Knowledge (another work), he would not have become a sinner. Clearly, Adam could be "saved" or lost only by works! To not work either way was to remain in the limbo of mere innocence. Faith or the lack thereof had nothing to do with the matter. In fact, Adam did not doubt what God had said about the tree in the least; *he knew he would die if he ate of it!* He believed God was telling him the truth. Thus Adam didn't have a lack of faith, he just had the wrong works.

At this point you may be thinking, "What about Romans 4, Galatians 2, Ephesians 2, and all the other passages which say works have nothing to do with salvation?" This is a good question, but be careful Christian; as we have stated before, don't assume everything found in the Bible applies doctrinally to everybody in every age. Romans, Galatians, Ephesians, and much of the rest of Paul's epistles apply to us today, but they *did not* apply to Adam. All Adam knew about these things was what God said to him in Genesis chapters 1 and 2, and we must not read anymore into it. If we read our doctrines back into his or any other's day, we wrest the Scriptures and end up with a doctrinal fantasy. Nowhere can we find where Adam was to have faith in anyone or believe in anyone, neither was the "new birth" or anything related to it even vaguely hinted at. *Everything hinged upon Adam's works.*

One can easily see how Adam's dispensational setup concerning salvation is drastically different to our's today. Now, salvation is a *free gift,* entirely by grace through faith apart from any works whatsoever. Furthermore, a born again believer is much more than just forgiven or innocent in God's sight, he is RIGHTEOUS. He has the imputed righteousness of his Savior Jesus Christ. God knew when he devised eternal salvation that man needed much more than just his sins forgiven and placed back into an innocent state, he needs the righteousness of his Son Jesus Christ. From this position the believer

CANNOT fall because he is in Christ and Christ is in him. God does not see the saved New Testament believer as only innocent (as Adam was), He sees him *positionally* with the perfect and spotless righteousness of the Lord Jesus Christ. *We receive much more in Christ than we lost in Adam (Rom. 5:20).*

After the fall things were much different for Adam and Eve. Their sin brought *guilt,* the guilt brought *shame,* and all three together brought *fear.* They were now truly lost, and the knowledge of it scared them. What could they do now? Their new knowledge did not supply the answer for this question. They tried to cover their sin with fig leaves, but that did not relieve their conscious of guilt. "What will God think when He sees us?"

The Lord was very gentle with His sinning creation. He did not consume them in His wrath or even belittle them. He just questioned them enough to get them to *confess* their sin and admit their guilt. After they confessed God offered His own covering for their sin in place of their self-righteous fig leaves, and they accepted. By doing so they abandoned their own means of dealing with sin for God's means, and that is all God asked of them. Here, however, we begin to see the entrance of faith concerning salvation. They did not need to have faith that God existed because He was right before them, but they did need to have faith in something God had *promised* to do. Of course, they were not to believe on someone who would die on a cross thousands of years later to redeem them from their sins, such a thing was unrevealed and unknown. All they knew was God was in some way going to send the **"seed"** of the woman to bruise the head of the serpent's seed and this would in some way deal with their sin and the curses. Looking forward to the "cross" is out of the question. All they knew was what God had shown and told them, nothing else. Of course, we today can look back and see the cross in Genesis 3:15 and 3:21, but this means nothing to Adam. He and Eve were saved by believing what God had *said* (faith) and by putting on the **"coats of skins"** God provided (works).

The coats of skins, which God obtained by killing the animals, showed Adam (and us) two very important lessons. First, God was willing to *provide salvation* to man; second, a *substitute* could purchase a sinner's salvation with its life. We can see these lessons very clearly now, but Adam did not have the advanced revelation we enjoy and was not certain of what all he observed meant.

Cain and Abel

After Adam and Eve were expelled from the Garden of Eden, God did not appear to them again. Since God no longer walked among His creation, faith came even more into play concerning His dealings with man. Cain and Abel were born after the expulsion and there is no record they ever saw God or heard Him speak (Cain did hear Him AFTER he offered his bloodless sacrifice). Apparently, all they knew of God was what they learned from their parents. When they went to offer sacrifices for their sins they were offering them by faith to a God they did not personally know, so their salvation, as well as (it appears) the salvation of all others in the *Dispensation of Conscience,* was based on faith along with an *element of works.* Abel had the right faith and the right works; Cain had some faith but the wrong works, but each must have works to be accepted.

God told Cain, **"If thou DOEST well, shalt thou not be accepted?"** (Gen. 4:7). Suppose Abel would have said, "I believe I am a sinner, and I believe God is willing to cover my sins if I offer a bloody substitute," but he did not offer the substitute, would he still be accepted? There is no indication he would have. He would have been in the same unaccepted condition as Cain. Along with his faith Abel had to perform the WORK of killing the offering and offer it to God before he would be respected (Gen. 4:4). As for Cain, he had faith that God existed (like the devils, Jam. 2:19), but he did not have the faith and works to present the proper sacrifice to God. Abel was respected by God because of faith and works, and Cain was rejected by the lack of the same. Either way works played a part in the salvation of many during this period.

From what the Scriptures reveal to us about the *Dispensation of Conscience,* every saved person in it was saved by grace through faith with works playing a part. Furthermore, with a few notable exceptions (which we will examine shortly) every saved person in the entire Old Testament was *saved by faith connected with works.* When people in the Old Testament were saved nothing happened IN them spiritually.

42

Of course, God imputed righteousness to their account when they obeyed him, but they were *not regenerated, a son of God, indwelt and sealed by the Holy Spirit, part of the body of Christ,* and the rest of the salvation doctrines unique to this age. Their sins were only *covered,* not taken away. In many ways they were saved on *credit* because Christ had not yet died on the cross to *purchase* their eternal redemption. But those in the *Dispensation of Conscience* knew practically none of this. Again, all they knew was what God had revealed up to that time as found in Genesis chapter 3:

- 1. Man is a sinner and doomed to death (3:7).
- 2. Man and the earth are cursed because of Adam's sin (3:17).
- 3. The woman's **"seed"** will bruise the head of the serpent's seed (they MAY have understood this to somehow relieve man of sin, death, and the curses), and the serpent's seed will bruise the woman's seed's heel (3:15).
- 4. Man has a knowledge of good and evil; a conscience that will excuse or convict his heart (3:5-6).
- 5. God will offer man a covering to cover his sin (3:21.
- 6. An animal substitute can supply the covering (3:21).

If God had other requirements of people during this dispensation they are not mentioned until we come to Noah. Reading New Testament doctrines into this time period brings nothing but confusion. Also, there is no reason to believe, or any verse to suggest that these people could not loose their salvation during this period. We will look more into this later, but nearly all of those saved in the Old Testament simply did not have anything *in* them (indwelling Holy Spirit) or any *promise* from God to permanently secure their salvation. Therefore, one could by faith (along with works) be saved and be on the right path toward "enduring to the end," and then, by a lack of faith fall away and loose all they gained. In a nutshell people are saved in every dispensation by simply doing what God SAYS. Sometimes it is works alone, sometimes faith alone, and sometimes both faith and works.

Noah and the Ark

Noah is the first person God gave a direct command to since Adam. Noah was found righteous (his own righteousness by works, not Christ's) by God among his generation of wickedness (Gen. 7:1), and God, by His grace, told him to build an ark to protect him from His wrath. With this command God added (to Noah and his family only) another requirement for salvation beside those so far revealed — to build an ark. Noah's faith is readily seen in his immediate obedience in beginning to build. He trusted God's word no matter how silly it may have sounded to others and went to work—*faith supplemented by works.* Here, some say, "The building of the ark was only for Noah's physical salvation, not his soul's salvation. He was saved only by faith." Really? Show us the chapter and verse that says so.

Where in Genesis chapters 1 through 7 can you find where Noah was saved by faith *alone?* Can't find it anyplace? How about searching the whole Bible, New Testament and all, for a verse that says Noah was saved by faith alone? Peter plainly says he was saved by water while in the ark (1 Pet. 3:20). You say, "Only his body was saved by water." Okay, PROVE IT with Scripture! If you can't you had better quit trusting someone else's opinion or your emotions for doctrine and begin trusting the Scriptures alone. Again, don't try to read Church Age doctrines into the past. John chapter 3 won't fit into Genesis chapter 6 no matter how hard you force it. If the ark had nothing to do with Noah's spiritual salvation, then the people who drowned in the flood may have been saved too, just not physically!

God told Noah to build an ark, and if he refused, he would have *drowned;* simple as that. Do you think he would have drowned saved? On what grounds? That Noah was found righteous (a righteousness based upon his OWN works relative to other men) at the beginning would mean nothing if he disobeyed a direct command from God; he would no longer be considered righteous. Since he refused to do what God said, he would likely perish just like the rest of the world. Unless God intervened and offered another means of salvation (as He did with Adam), Noah would have died lost—an unrepentant sinner. His quick obedience in building the ark, however, proved he had the proper faith. Faith supplemented by works. Today, saved people can refuse to do what God has commanded and they DON'T forfeit their salvation. Millions of regenerated believers disobey God's commands and their salvation is unaffected. Why? The difference is in the dispensations and also in what happens INSIDE the believer. You should be beginning to see, Christian, how you have a much more gracious age to live under with much better promises to claim than those of the past. We have many more privileges than Noah, but with the privileges come responsibilities.

Faithful Abraham

Now we come to Abraham, and he is an interesting case. With him God introduces the first instance of salvation ONLY by faith. Not New Testament salvation by a long shot, but salvation by faith. Abraham is known as **"faithful Abraham"** because of his great faith in God, but his faith was not *always* great. When God first spoke to him, his faith was not even enough to save him! Many forget that when Abraham obeyed God and went into the land as God commanded (Gen. 12), he wasn't saved. He didn't get saved until Genesis 15:6, several years later! All through chapters 12, 13, 14, and the first few verses of 15, Abraham was dead lost! Before he was saved Abraham had works, he forsook his homeland and moved to Canaan, and he had some faith, he believed God enough to go, but he did not have enough or the right kind of faith for God to save him until Genesis chapter 15.

In Genesis 15:6 Abraham finally exercised enough faith in what God had said and was saved. Before he heard the promises of having descendants and becoming a great nation, but he didn't fully believe them until chapter 15. God was showing Abraham that He was capable of keeping His word and was worthy to be trusted. In a larger sense God was showing mankind that no matter how great and seemingly unlikely to be fulfilled His promises are, He is fully capable of keeping them. Abraham was the first to trust God this far, and spiritually he is the "father" of all who exercise like faith and believe God for salvation.

Abraham's salvation is like ours today in only one respect: he was saved **"by grace through faith"** apart from works with *righteousness* *imputed* to his account. To receive salvation Abraham simply took God at His word. His faith and the faith of believers today is the same kind and in the same God, but here the similarities end. What Abraham believed God would do is drastically different from what one is to believe today. Abraham believed his **"seed"** would number as the stars in heaven, and God saved him for it. He believed nothing about someone dying on a cross for his sins or anything like that, he could only believe in what God had revealed to him. Furthermore, to show how different his salvation is from a believer's today note:

- Abraham was not *regenerated or born again.* Nothing happened inside him when he was saved. Dozens of things happen in a born again Christian.
- He was not a *"son of God."* Since he was not *"born of God"* he could not be a son of God, neither could he ever call God his *father.*
- He did not receive the Holy Spirit *permanently* to indwell or seal him.
- He was not placed *in Christ* nor was Christ in him.
- He did not receive a *new nature.* All he ever had was the Adamic nature.
- He had no *completed atonement* to eternally redeem him.
- He did not go to *Heaven* when he died.

Though Abraham was saved by faith as we are today, clearly the salvation his faith brought him is not the same salvation we presently enjoy. James even tell us that Abraham's *justification* was not completed until he offered Isaac up in Genesis 22 (James 2:21)! He was imputed righteousness in chapter 15 and thus saved, but he was not *fully* justified until he performed the WORK of offering Isaac in chapter 22. James doesn't hesitate to tell us Abraham was *justified by works* after he was saved (James 2:21). On the contrary a believer today is justified the instant he trusts Christ for his salvation. All of the eternal aspects of salvation occur instantly and simultaneously when he believes. Paul, in Romans and Galatians, uses Abraham as a figure of Church Age salvation, but he is only that, a *figure;* not an exact picture. Abraham was saved when he believed God was going to do something He SAID He would do (Rom. 4:20-22), and so are we saved, but again, what we are to believe is very different from what Abraham believed.

Suppose someone today sincerely believed God would give him descendants that number as the stars of heaven as the basis of his salvation, would such faith save him? Hardly. No matter how much he believed it he would remain lost. Not because he didn't have enough faith, but because he had it in the wrong promise. God has revealed much more to man since the days of Abraham, and man is required to believe and act on the more recent revelation (Jesus Christ) to be saved. At this point you may be thinking, "Yes, but Christ said Himself that Abraham saw His day and was glad (John 8:56), so he must have believed on Christ." Now wait a minute. First of all Christ's words refer to Genesis 22 when Isaac was offered, not Genesis 15 when Abraham was saved; and second, Abraham did not in some supernatural sense gaze into the future and see Christ on the cross. He saw Christ's day in that he believed Isaac would be resurrected from death, not by supposedly seeing the future crucifixion of the Son of God by a miraculous vision.

Abraham not only believed God was able to resurrect Isaac, he believed God WOULD resurrect him after he was slain! He was glad because by faith he saw the resurrection of his **"seed"** and was *convinced* God would fulfill all of His promises to him through this resurrected seed. Abraham saw in Isaac a figure of a **"son"** slain because of sin and later resurrected, but he did not see the figure fulfilled in Christ. Of course, with the Scriptures as hindsight, we can see both clearly.

Abraham's Seed

From Abraham on the opportunity for salvation belonged only to one family at the exclusion of all others. Christ said **"salvation is of the Jews"** (John 4:22), and Abraham is the first Jew. He was saved while still a Gentile (Rom. 4), but when the covenant was sealed with the sign of circumcision (Gen. 17), Abraham became the first Jew. The Lord told Abraham **"in Isaac shall thy seed be called,"** so Isaac inherited his promises. Isaac likely believed the promises as much as his father. This is indicated in Genesis 22 where he allows Abraham to bind him for a burnt offering. Since Abraham was an old man and Isaac a youth, it is not likely Abraham could have tied Isaac up if Isaac would not have allowed him. He loved his father and also had faith in his father's God, believing that he would yet live.

Isaac's son Jacob also desired the promises. This is evident when he bought his brother Esau's birthright for a bowl of pottage. Even though Jacob was a **"supplanter"** and **"deceiver"** most of his life, he still had an eye for the promises God gave to his fathers (Gen. 28:10-22; 35:9-15). Esau, the first born, did not think the birthright was worth much or he wouldn't have sold it. That God would later identify Himself to Moses as the God of **"Abraham, Isaac, and Jacob"** testifies of their saving faith in Him. Because of their faith all three of them are still alive even though they are physically dead, for **"God is not the God of the dead but of the living"** (Matt. 22:32).

Jacob's twelve sons further inherit the promises and become the twelve tribes of Israel. How many of these twelve and their descendants in Egypt trusted God for the promises is unknown. Certainly Joseph did, and likely most or all of his brethren, but we know of no passage that proves it. The Bible doesn't tell us everything we may like to know, but it tells us everything we NEED to know. Every believer must be careful not to let *emotion or opinion* influence his quest for sound doctrine. Assumed doctrines nearly always lead to heresy, so if a believer can't reasonably show something is true with Scripture, don't assume it is true just because it sounds "scholarly."

In summary, salvation during the 2500 years from Adam to Moses was by grace through faith with works *indicating and fulfilling the faith*. There was no new birth then or any of the Church Age doctrines that go with it because it was not yet available (John 7:39). Neither did those saved go to Heaven when they died (with the exception of Enoch and later Elijah who are special cases). Though faith was to be in God, it had to be in a promise God had revealed. To believe God existed was not enough; *one had to believe and act upon what God had revealed to him* for the person to be saved. What God said to Adam, He didn't say to Abel; what He commanded Noah (ark), He did not command Abraham, etc. Each person had to believe what was relevant to him.

As for works God required a certain degree of *personal righteousness* of all (Noah preached righteousness while building the ark, 2 Pet. 2:5), and also obedience of any personal commands He might give. At least up until Abraham, to *only believe* the revelations, commands, and promises was not sufficient, each person had to *act on them* and *continue* doing so, to secure his salvation. As in every age each individual is responsible for following his conscience and coming to God for salvation when he realizes he has broken it (Rom. 2:15). Faith was, of course, the major component in this salvation equation, but for many works were also essential. The works were really an indicator the person had the right faith. If a person had faith but was *unable* to perform the works (sacrifice, etc.), God likely took this into consideration. But if a person acted like he had faith and really didn't and still performed works (like Cain), he remained lost. Faith had to come first, and it motivated the works. Of the millions of people who lived during this period (around 2500 years), we can only find two or three dozen in the Scriptures we can say with any assurance were truly saved.

The method of salvation during this period was not fixed; each person's responsibility was simply to *do what God said.* As we have seen God required different things of different people, unlike today where every Christian is saved by believing a consistent gospel. Again, there are not as many details in the Bible as we may like to have concerning salvation before the cross, but enough is there for us to see how it is different from our's today. This will be further manifested in the next section where we look at salvation in the *Dispensation of Law* under the *Mosaic Covenant.*

Moses the Law Giver

As mentioned in the last chapter, while they were in Egypt the descendants of Abraham grew into millions. During this time they were still under the *Dispensation of Promise,* and there is no record that God revealed anything new to them until Moses came along. After He commissioned Moses to go back to Egypt and speak in His behalf, God began to reveal Himself to His people again. Through Moses He showed both the Israelites and Egyptians His great power with the ten plagues and the parting of the Red Sea. He also showed His love and concern for Israel by offering them a way to avoid the destroyer at the first **"Passover."**

God's requirements of the Israelites at the first Passover (Ex. 12) plainly show how works were involved in their salvation. No matter how much faith each Israelite had, if he neglected to put the lamb's blood above and beside the door, the firstborn in the house was doomed to death. God told them in no uncertain terms they MUST APPLY the blood (works) before He would pass over them (Ex. 12:13). Faith alone was not enough (Ex. 12:7)! It is true their salvation was based on faith in the shed blood of a lamb, but until the blood was *applied* as required, the faith was ineffective for the salvation of the firstborn. Today, Christ Himself (who is the fulfillment of the Passover figure), through the Holy Spirit, does the work of applying His blood to the believer. The first Passover is one of the strongest indications that under Law certain works were a requirement for salvation.

The physical salvation of the firstborn during the Passover was a *picture* of the spiritual salvation of each individual Jew during the *Dispensation of Law*. It testifies, again, that one is saved by doing what God has said to do. Nearly 1500 years later the Passover is revealed as a picture of the **"lamb of God which taketh away the sins of the world,"** but, again, this was unknown to the Israelites in Egypt. They were passed over only because they did what God told them to do They didn't fully understand the Passover's present meaning and had no knowledge at all of its future significance. The Passover was preparing the Israelites for the new covenant God would make with them in Exodus 19, which was *solely conditioned on works.*

After leading them out of Egypt and providing their every need in the wilderness, God officially established His covenant with them at Mt. Sinai. Again, this covenant is conditioned entirely upon works. Israel as a nation and also each individual was to keep all the requirements of the law, and when they failed, offer the proper sacrifice or possibly forfeit their salvation. The punishment for individuals who failed to obey was being **"cut off from among his people"** (Ex. 31:14). This "cutting off" was often physical death (Num. 9:13; 15:30-31), but more than that it was being cut off from *the promises and covenant connected with Israel.* In effect, *cut off from salvation* or the opportunity to obtain it. We will see as we go along that works play a larger role concerning salvation under the Law than it did before.

The *Mosaic Covenant* and the *Dispensation of Law* was for the most part a series of *rules, regulations, conditional blessings, curses, laws, statutes, commandments, memorials, etc.*, which were in the larger sense designed to show man his evil nature and sin (Rom. 3:20). But to the Israelites of the time it was a religious system based on strict obedience with little or no mercy for the lawbreaker. Paul said it was **"not of faith, but the man that DOETH them shall live by them"** (Gal. 3:12), indicating its demand for obedience. Faith alone could not deliver the **"sinner."** In fact, **"faith"** is only found two times in the whole Old Testament (Deut. 32:20; Hab. 2:4), and in both places it refers to a *man's own faith,* not the saving faith God provides believers today (Eph. 2:8-9).

What God demanded of Israel was for them to do what they promised at Sinai (Ex. 19, see chapter 1), obey His every word. If they obeyed as a nation, He cared for and blessed them as a nation; if they refused, He eventually cursed and scattered them. This is clear in Deuteronomy chapters 28-30. Concerning individuals, however, salvation was not so clear. If an Israelite (or proselyte) feared God, wanted to please Him by trying to obey all His laws, and offered the proper sacrifices when he failed, at that moment one could assume he was in a saved state. Unlike today, there was no clear and simple faith "formula" given. Since nothing spiritually happened inside these people to "preserve" them and they had no promise of security to claim, their salvation was not unconditionally permanent. It appears if one at any time had a *lack of faith, works, or both to a certain degree, his salvation was in jeopardy.* Only God knew who was saved for certain at any given time. The individual in most cases likely did not know exactly where he stood regarding his salvation. At one point God told Elijah only 7000 Jews had not bowed their knee to Baal out of all the millions of Israel. The others had broken the covenant and apparently forfeited their salvation (if they had it to start with) by worshipping a false god.

When works are involved in salvation it is difficult to know where one stands with God. The person seldom, if ever, had complete assurance that he was accepted because a future failure could cost him everything. All he could do was trust in God and to the best of his ability do what God required of him. When he failed he must repent, offer the appropriate sacrifice, and beseech God for forgiveness and restoration (Psalm 51). In contrast, every believer today can have absolute assurance of salvation because he is not trusting any in his works but in the shed blood and works of another, his Lord Jesus Christ

In Exodus 34:6-7 God told Moses concerning salvation He was **"merciful and gracious, longsuffering and abundant in goodness and truth, keeping mercy for thousands, forgiving inequity and transgression and sin...,"** but the Lord goes on to say that all of these blessings **"...will by no means CLEAR the guilty"**! In the Old Testament when someone was saved and forgiven according to God's mercy, grace, longsuffering, goodness, truth, etc., he was still not cleared from his guilt. This is an important lesson. *Remission and forgiveness of sins is NOT redemption.* In the Old Testament God did forgive people and treat them as such but only with a view of the redemption Christ would later purchase on Calvary (Rom. 3:25). With the atonement that could "take away" their sins and clear them not yet available, salvation was only a decree, and the individuals remained inherently guilty. They were only forgiven sinners, not regenerated, justified, redeemed Christians. This is the main reason Old Testament saints didn't go to Heaven at death. Even though righteousness was imputed to their account, they were still in every other way guilty sinners.

The best way to see how salvation worked under the Law is to examine the lives of some people who lived during that period and study what the Scriptures reveal. Again, salvation is somewhat elusive and hard to consistently pin down under the Law, but the study of a few representative individuals will help one understand how different it is from Church Age salvation. Clear statements of salvation, like Abraham's (Gen. 15:6), are very rare under the Law. For the most part one is only left to assume the salvation of many individuals by noting circumstantial evidence that suggests (but does not prove) their salvation. One can conclusively prove the salvation of very few people in the entire Old Testament.

Aaron

The first time Aaron, the onetime High Priest, is mentioned in the Bible is when God rebukes Moses for trying to get out of his commission to deliver the Israelites in Exodus chapter 4. Because of his complaining, God told Moses his brother Aaron would be his mouth and speak what God had spoken to him (Ex. 4:16, 30). After Moses came down from Sinai, Aaron met him and Moses relayed to Aaron all God had said to him (vs.28). Aaron received the words of the Lord and accepted his commission from God to be Moses' spokesperson. When they returned to Egypt, **"Aaron spake all the words the Lord had spoken unto Moses, and did the signs in the sight of the people. And the people believed..."** (vs. 30-31). Everything in the chapter indicates Aaron (along with Moses) is saved. He obeyed the Lord in going into the wilderness to seek Moses (vs. 27); he received God's word through Moses (vs. 28); and he did the work of speaking God's word and performing the signs (vs. 30). It appears he did everything he knew to do and all that God had reveled for him to do. From this we may reasonably assume he was saved; not born again, but saved in the Old Testament sense.

While he was in Egypt, Aaron saw God do many mighty things through himself and Moses. He saw firsthand the character, power, and salvation of the Lord and took part in the greatest Exodus in history. Everything was looking good, but a few weeks later when they were in the wilderness, things changed. After God had made His covenant with Israel (Ex. 19) and revealed His laws (Ex. 20-24), Moses again went up to Sinai for more instructions (Ex. 24:18). While he was on the mount **"the people"** got restless, and they demanded Aaron to make them **"gods"** to worship (Ex. 32:1). (Man must worship something. If he refuses to worship the true God, he will worship a false one, even if it is himself!) After all he had seen and all God had done through him and for him, Aaron was quick to entertain Israel's idolatry and instructed them to bring gold. Out of this gold he made a calf and the people said, **"These be thy gods, O Israel,"** and they had a feast and offered the calf a burnt offering (Ex. 32:4). How quickly Israel and Aaron abandoned their God.

The Lord told Moses what Israel was doing, and filled with wrath He was ready to *consume* the whole nation (Ex. 32:10). Furthermore, He was especially angry with Aaron, enough to destroy him (Deut. 9:20). *Now, what about Aaron's salvation?* Could someone who readily broke the first two commandments still be saved? Even though Aaron may have been coerced into the situation, he still chose to encourage the people in their idolatry rather than rebuke them. Moses brought up the promises God had previously made and the Lord repented of offering to consume Israel, including Aaron, but after Moses came down and saw the idolatry himself, *he too* was filled with wrath (Ex. 32:19)! Moses confronted his brother, and Aaron, afraid, tried to wiggle out of the blame (vs. 22), but the damage was done. Moses charges Aaron with bringing a great sin upon Israel.

If Aaron died at this time, *where would he go?* Are you sure (chapter and verse)? Moses knew the dire consequences of this sin and was willing to have his *name blotted out of God's book* if it would atone for Israel, including Aaron (Ex. 32:32). Moses' actions indicate that the salvation of all those involved was on precarious ground since he was apparently *willing to sacrifice his salvation for theirs.* They had either lost their salvation or were on the verge of losing it because God said He would only blot out those who sinned against Him (vs. 33). What a harrowing thought, to have one's name blotted out of God's book, *but God said He WOULD do it!* At least some names *were* blotted out! In Psalm 69:28 this book is called the "book of the living" and is connected with righteousness. Furthermore, this book must also concern spiritual life after death, not just physical life. Remember, **"God is not the God of the dead, but of the living."**

As for Aaron, however, we still can't prove he lost his salvation. Yes, he was among those who greatly sinned against God, but, also, he was of the tribe of Levi and among those who went out and slew his brother, companion, and neighbor (Ex. 32:27-29), indicating he was again on the Lord's side. Killing one's family and friends if need be would require much consecration (vs. 29), and apparently Aaron had it. He knew what he did was wrong, but when given the opportunity to do right he repented and joined with those who follow the Lord. Needless to say Aaron was not killed that day, but the status of his salvation during his great sin is unknown.

Maybe Aaron lost his salvation when he made the calf (a lack of faith, and the wrong works) and gained it back when he fought on the Lord's side. Maybe he didn't lose it at all, but apparently about 3000 did and died that way (vs. 28, 33)! If God blotted them out of his book and they died in that condition, they were certainly lost. See what we mean when we say salvation under the Law is indefinite and "shifty"? Many today may arrogantly claim, "Of course Aaron was saved, and it was impossible for him to loose his salvation because Romans chapter 3 says... etc. etc.," but this PROVES nothing. We are interested in what the Bible says, not in the opinions of someone who refuses to divide the Scriptures or is guided more by emotions and "historic positions" than a desire for the truth.

God, again, graciously used Aaron (as High Priest) in spite of the events in Exodus 32, and after serving Him for 40 years Aaron was stripped of his priestly garments and sent to the top of Mt. Hor to die. God told Moses Aaron would be **"gathered unto his people"** (Num. 20:24) just like Abraham was and Moses was later (Deut. 32:50). So, in the end, everything indicates Aaron died saved and right with God; but if he died that idolatrous day at Sinai, the Lord only knows.

Samson

Next we will briefly look at Samson, the judge of Israel. As far as works are concerned Samson had plenty, but they were nearly all bad. He sought a heathen Philistine woman and married her (Judges 14:1); he broke his Nazerite vows by touching dead bodies and not offering a sacrifice to remove his uncleanness (14:6); he killed 30 men only for their clothes (14:19); he went in unto a harlot (16:1); he later went unto another woman—Delilah (16:4); he led to Delilah (16:7, 11); he revealed the secret of his strength (16:17); and finally committed suicide (16:30). Not particularly a model life to follow.

God was long-suffering and put up with Samson's "indiscretions," but when he gave up the secret of his strength, *God left him* (Jud. 16:20)! Even though Samson was a conceited, self-indulgent, self-gratifying, woman-chaser nearly all his life, his name is recorded with the *heroes of faith* in Hebrews 11. The only time he called upon God for anything other than right before his death was because he was thirsty (15:18), yet he is recorded among the most faithful in history. Fascinating. How are we to understand this? Of course, only by grace.

God was exceedingly gracious to Samson. He gave him many opportunities to serve Him and was very patient with his behavior, but when his hair was cut, in essence dissolving his Nazarite relationship with God, God left him. The Scriptures plainly say, **"...the Lord was departed from him."** Now, was Samson still saved? Can you prove it? Nearly everything he did in the past was from a selfish or vengeful motive. Furthermore, he despised his Nazarite position and neglected to remove his uncleanness and guilt with the proper sacrifices, then he allowed his hair to be cut. Was he saved while the Lord was departed from him? God only knows, but the tone of the passage is not very promising. However, in faith Samson repents (16:28) and begs God to remember him by returning and restoring his strength. Here, the right faith is seen, and if he lost his salvation, it was returned. We know he died saved from Hebrews 11:32.

Saul

Saul, Israel's first king, is also an interesting case. After Israel rejected the Lord and wanted a human king to reign over them, God told Samuel to anoint Saul (1 Sam. 9:16). In the beginning Saul was meek and humble (9:21), and shortly after he was anointed the spirit of the Lord came upon him and he prophesied among prophets (10:6) God also gave him another heart. At the same time Samuel told him, **"God is with thee"** (10:7). Saul became highly esteemed by Israel and they considered him a prophet (10:12). Up to this point everything is positive concerning Saul, but was he saved? The evidence so far would indicate he was. He had the *Holy Spirit, prophesied, and God was with him;* a good testimony for anyone, but let's go on.

After following the Holy Spirit and defeating the Ammonites (11:6), Saul's character began to change. First, he usurped the office of a priest by offering a sacrifice himself (13:9), then he made a rash and senseless vow causing Israel to sin and jeopardizing his son Jonathan's life (14:24, 32, 44), and after that he refused to strictly follow God's command to **"utterly destroy"** Ameleck (15:3, 9). As a result of this God rejected him as king (15:23) and took the Holy Spirit away from him replacing Him with a devil (16:14). The rest of Saul's life was spent trying to recapture what he had lost through disobedience. He relentlessly pursues David, his soon to be successor, and after consulting a witch (28:8), finally dies of suicide on a Philistine battlefield (31:4). Did Saul die saved? God only knows.

The Lord told David He took His MERCY from Saul (2 Sam. 7:15). This is not at all a good sign. On the other hand, Samuel told Saul that when he died he would be with him (1 Sam. 28:19, and, of course, Samuel is saved (Heb. 11:32). However, Samuel may have only meant Saul would be with him in death, not in the same place or state as he after death. We cannot prove it either way. When Saul was on the right path and in fellowship with God it would be very reasonable to conclude he was saved. But when he rebelled and forsook God's ways, he may have fell from his "saved" state. During the latter part of his life he had very little faith. The Holy Spirit left Saul never to return (except to protect David 1 Sam. 19:23); *Christian, can He leave YOU* (Eph. 4:30)? Anyone who says salvation is the same in the Old Testament as it is in the New Testament is simply ignorant of the Scriptures.

Joab

Another interesting character is Joab, David's nephew and top general. Joab is not portrayed in the Scriptures as a very spiritual person. He is not revealed as a man of prayer or Godward devotion, and he, for the most part, only speaks of God when it will further his cause. Joab was very ambitious and ruthlessly stepped on anyone who stood in the way of his lust for power. He would not even hesitate to murder if it would protect his position. Besides murdering Abner (2 Sam. 3:27) and Amasa (20:10) in cold blood; he caused the death of Uriah (and others) by sending him into a foolish battle for the sole purpose of getting him killed (11:16-17); he defied David's orders and killed Absalom (18:14); and he threatened and treated David with disrespect (19:6-7). These are just some of his wicked acts. Clearly, Joab is not someone to emulate.

However, after Solomon became king, Joab suddenly became "religious." When David was near the end of his days, his eldest son, Adonijah, wanted to be king (1 Ki. 1:5) and Joab joined him in his attempt (1:7). David got wind of Adonijah's plan and quickly crowned Solomon king (1:43), putting Joab on the wrong side. With David's sudden abdication and the crowning of Solomon, Joab knew he was in a "pickle." With all his past actions and his present allegiance to Adonijah, he knew his life wouldn't be very highly esteemed (2:5-6).

After Solomon had Adonijah killed, Joab, believing he would be next, ran to the tabernacle, grabbed hold of the horns of the alter, and, in effect, *pled the blood!* He went there as a place of sanctuary, hoping to receive mercy (like Adonijah had previously), but Solomon had him killed on the spot (2:31). There is very little to indicate the salvation of Joab until he asks for mercy at the brazen alter. Was he saved there? He appeared to be trusting in the blood of the substitute lamb that was burning on the alter and wanted to die beside it (2:30)? *This is as close as it gets to "looking forward to the cross"* in the Old Testament, but apparently his **"faith"** wasn't enough. Joab did not receive the Holy Spirit and is not said to **"sleep with his fathers"** as David or be **"gathered unto his people"** like Abraham. He is only referred to as dead (11:21) like the **"rich man"** in Luke 16:22.

David

The last Old Testament person we will look at, though we could examine several more, is David—**"a man after God's own heart."** Of course, David's salvation is beyond question in spite of all his failures, but we will see David is a special case. David appears to be saved from his first mention in the Bible. The Holy Spirit came on him when he was anointed to be king and never left him the rest of his life (1 Sam. 16:13). Furthermore, his first words show his confidence in the **"living God"** (17:26), and he credits God for his deliverance from the lion and the bear (17:37). Everything seemed fine between him and God. Later, though, while he was being pursued by Saul, David began to doubt God's promise for him to be king (20:3). He consequently began to make some serious spiritual mistakes (21:2; etc.).

Even with the doubt and resulting sins, though, David still mostly trusted God and respected His will (24:6-12), and God continued to bless and protect him.

When David was finally made king, he reigned with prudence and wisdom, and God made the previously mentioned unconditional and far-reaching covenant with him concerning his kingdom and seed (2 Sam. 7). Again, everything was going well for David; that is, until he *eyed Bathsheba* (11:2).

The events concerning Bathsheba led David to commit adultery and murder; two sins no animal sacrifice will atone for. Those were both capital crimes against God's law and demanded death (Lev. 20:10; Num. 35:30-32). David knew faith in the shed blood of the lamb would not redeem him (Psa. 51:16), and he didn't even attempt to offer it. When confronted with his unpardonable sins, David confessed and repented and God did not require his life (2 Sam. 12:13). Ordinarily, repentance or no repentance, the adulterer and murderer must die (Lev. 20:10; Ex. 21:14); but God, by His abundant grace, spared David. This shows that David is an *exceptional case* in the Old Testament, not typical at all. For His own reasons God granted David **"sure mercies"** (Acts 13:34); the closest thing one will find to eternal security in the Old Testament. Remember how God took His mercy from Saul in 2 Sam. 7:15 and then promised David He wouldn't take his mercy from his seed? There is clearly a difference, and it is by grace—pure grace. David is a type of the New Testament Church Age believer. Still, David was NOT born again, sealed by the Holy Spirit, or made a new creature in Christ; he simply had a *promise* from God of **"sure mercies,"** and this promise secured his salvation.

Whether David fully understood these **"sure mercies"** is not clear, but understanding them is not necessary for them to be effective. Many today do not realize the riches of the salvation they have, but, nevertheless, the riches are still there. David did know, however, that the Holy Spirit *could be taken* from him and he begged God not to do it (Psa. 51:11). He knew his sins warranted such action, but he dreaded the thought of losing his precious comforter which represented communion and fellowship with God. This great dread of losing the Holy Spirit is one reason David is called **"a man after God's own heart."** As many of his psalms testify, he dearly loved the things of

God and the presence of God. Obviously, David is an exception to the rule dealing with salvation under the Law. He was given **"exceedingly great and precious promises"** that God did not give to any other person in the Old Testament, including Abraham and Moses.

See how hard it is to pin salvation down under the Law? We can look at the apostle Paul and see clearly where he was saved in Acts 9; we have no problem seeing 3000 others get saved on the day of Pentecost in Acts 2; we can with the utmost confidence believe every-one who receives Jesus Christ in him has eternal, everlasting life, but the salvation of many prominent characters in the Old Testament is hard to positively determine.

Remember, in the Old Testament salvation was an EXTERNAL decree by God when certain conditions were met; it was not finalized until Christ purchased eternal redemption at Calvary. Church Age salvation is an INTERNAL act of regeneration performed by the permanently indwelling Christ through the Holy Spirit. The external decree of salvation could be rescinded because of disobedience or rebellion, but the internal new birth cannot be undone. The former salvation is indefinite and variable according to God's good pleasure, and the latter is permanent, invariable, and fixed because of God's good pleasure. Who are we to take issue with God's methods? Our duty is not to question but believe and obey all that He says.

The five individual cases we have examined above reveal how varied salvation could be under the law. Faith had a part, and works had a part, but only God determined how much of each He required to decree each person saved. There were no fixed requirements. God evidently took many things into consideration before salvation was decreed: what had been revealed to the person, how much "light" the person had, how much opportunity the person had to do what was required, what the person did with what he knew, etc. God is a God of mercy and grace, but still, His justice and holiness must be satis-fied. Since there was no new birth to distinguish the lost from the saved, God saved those who did (and continued to do) what He said.

At first it appears *Aaron* had the proper faith and acceptable works, but at Sinai he lacked both. *Samson* had the Holy Spirit, but after many evil works He left him; however, after he exercised faith, the Holy Spirit returned. *Saul* had some good works but a lack of faith, and the Holy Spirit left him never to return. *Joab* had a little faith and evil works but in the end went to the altar to "plead the blood" for mercy. And *David* had some evil works and unbelief, but at other times he had good works and much faith. He further prayed that the Holy Spirit would not leave him, and He never did. What a collage of "experiences." The Holy Spirit *leaves one and later returns; He leaves another but does not return; and He could have left a third but didn't!* Does this sound anything like New Testament salvation? How could anyone say salvation is the same in the Old Testament as in the New?

In summary, salvation under the Law was fundamentally different from our's today. Then, faith backed by works were required; today, *faith alone* is sufficient. Then, nothing spiritual happened inside a believer; today, *many things happen.* Then, salvation was only decreed on credit; today, it is *internally and spiritually applied.* Then, believers didn't go to heaven when they died; today, *all believers go there.* Then, the Holy Spirit did not permanently indwell and seal believers; today, *He does both. etc. etc.* Do you now see the fallacy of those who claim salvation in every age is the same? It is not even the same between different dispensations in the Old Testament, let alone the same as today's.

David's son, Solomon (who after years of faithfulness forsook God and worshipped devils [1 Kings 11] and died leaving no record of ever having repented! Another interesting case), spoke the definitive statement concerning Old Testament Salvation. In Ecclesiastes 12:13 he said, **"Fear God, and keep his commandments: for this is the whole duty of man."** No mention of a redeemer or cross; no mention of redemption or regeneration; no mention of believing on or receiving anybody; just fear God and keep His commandments. What commandments? Whatever ones God has revealed and made valid for the person and time. This is as plain as it gets (see also Micah 6:7-8).

In the next chapter we will move into the New Testament and examine salvation there. We will look at the transitional change from the Law to Grace and study the changes in salvation this new dispensation brought about.

Chapter III
Salvation In The New Testament

As mentioned in the last chapter, salvation was only decreed to those saved in the Old Testament because the necessary atonement and redemption to take the sins away had not yet been made (Heb. 10:4). Only the **"lamb of God,"** Jesus Christ, who came in the **"fullness of time"** (Gal. 4:4) could make an acceptable atonement and provide **"eternal redemption"** to forever remove the penalty and guilt of sin from any believer. The hundreds of thousands of bloody animal sacrifices offered to God in the Old Testament could not do this, they could only temporarily cover the sins until Christ's expiatory sacrifice took them away. God decreed salvation to people in the Old Testament and remitted their sins solely on the basis of what He knew Christ would later do on the cross (Rom. 3:25).

Christ said Himself He came to die **"for** (because of) **the remission of sins"** in the past (Matt. 26:28). Without the cross God's decree of salvation would be of no lasting effect; God had to ultimately purchase eternal redemption. Thus the whole religious system of Judaism as revealed in the Old Testament could eternally save no one. It was for the most part a great object lesson to show man *he was a sinner* (Rom. 3:20), *sin required payment* (death) (Lev. 1-15), *and a substitute provided by God could die in the sinner's place* (Ex. 12). By the time Jesus was born, God had spent 4000 years trying to get these basic and essential doctrines through man's stubborn head, insisting man cannot save himself and only God can provide escape from the everlasting penalty of sin and supply eternal salvation.

Hebrews 10:6-8 says God took no pleasure in the animal sacrifices He required; they could not effectually deal with sin and neither could they satisfy God's justice and holiness. Only another man could pay for man's sin, and for this reason God prepared a body for the Word to become flesh. The eternal Word was **"made of a woman, made under the law, to redeem them that were under the law..."** (Gal. 4:4-5) and came **"in the likeness of sinful flesh"** (Rom. 8:3) so He could permanently redeem those born of Adam who will receive

Him. Not only did God become a man to redeem mankind, He also came to earth as a man (not just in a man's body, but born fully a man) because He wanted to express and reveal Himself to man. This is why Christ is referred to as **"the Word"** (John 1:1); He is God's means of communicating Himself. God wanted man to know what kind of a person He is.

The animal sacrifices in the Old Testament were only a shadow of Christ's redemptive work (Heb. 10:1). And if God took no pleasure in the death of the animal sacrifices, how much less the death of His Son? His Son is infinity more valuable than any man, group of men, or animal, yet He gave His Son anyway. Contrary to today's popular self-esteem—self-worth "theology," man is by no means worth the suffering, agony, and separation from His Father Christ endured to redeem him, but God paid it nonetheless. Why? *Simply because His LOVE and GRACE compelled Him to.* God by His nature loved rebellious man immensely and motivated by this love devised a redemption plan to rescue him from his sins. Concerning salvation man can take credit for nothing. Individually or collectively man is not worth the price; it is all of God. God loves us not because of who we are, *but because of who HE is!* The self-esteem nuts who think otherwise are blinded by their bloated egos.

All of God's moral attributes were seen at the cross. His *mercy* was seen in allowing sinful man to live; His *grace* was seen which favored man with an opportunity to be redeemed; His *justice* and *holiness* were satisfied by Christ's propitiatory death; His *righteousness* was seen in Christ's righteous life and death; etc., but all of this was motivated by His unequaled *love.* God could have let man fall into Hell and pay for his sins himself throughout eternity and all of His attributes would have been satisfied, except for Mercy, Grace and Love. With the cross they ALL are satisfied. What a great God is our God! A God who gave Himself to redeem His enemies (Rom. 5:10)! Praise His name!

Every person ever saved in any dispensation is redeemed by Christ's death and shed blood. Though people in the various dispensations are saved differently concerning what is required of them to receive salvation, the *basis* of all salvation regardless of time or place is the blood of Christ. Without the blood no matter what one believed or did to be saved he would remain **"without hope and without God"** and be left to pay for his sins himself. In this chapter we will not emphasize the salvation doctrines of this present Church Age because they should be well know to the reader if he has been a Christian long (see the author's book on the *Eight Major Doctrines of Salvation* entitled *More Than Forgiven* for a concise study of these doctrines). Rather we are mainly going to examine the transition from "Law" to "Grace" and from "Grace" to the future dispensations, making every effort to rightly divide the Scriptures along the way.

The Old Testament In The New

One of the most common mistakes people make in studying the Bible is assuming all the books called the New Testament doctrinally refer to the *Dispensation of Grace.* In fact, nearly all the events recorded in the four gospels occurred under the *Law,* not under *Grace.* The New Testament was not established until the crucifixion (Matt. 27; Mark 15; Luke 23; John 19) so everything that happened before then was doctrinally under the Law. Remember how Christ was made under the law so He could redeem them that were under the law (Gal. 4)? Christ was born, lived, and died under the dominion of the Law of Moses. He said Himself He came **"not to destroy the law but fulfill"** (Matt. 5:17), indicating His subjection to it. Realizing this should help one understand many passages found in the gospels (and also in Hebrews and Revelation) that indicate someone can lose his salvation or standing before God. Many today who don't understand these passages use them to teach a born again Christian can lose his salva-tion. Usually a person will only be saved a short while before one of these "Endurers" (one who believes a person must "endure to the end" to be saved) pulls out a verse to "prove" he can "lose it." Interestingly enough these people do not have to use a source other than the Bible to promote this doctrine because the Bible can be their greatest ally. Their error is not that they don't believe the Bible, it is that they fail to rightly divide it.

Since the Reformation there has only been two groups of Chris-tians that have consistently believed a born again Christian could not lose his salvation—the *Baptists* and the *Presbyterians.* Every other denomination (Methodists, Lutherans, Anglicans, Greek Orthodox, Roman Catholics, etc.) believe a Christian can do something to forfeit his salvation. This includes the newer denominations (Pentecostal, Church of Christ, etc.) and the cults. These "Arminian" groups will disagree among each other on many things, but they all agree that a regenerated, justified, redeemed Christian can fall from his salvation and go to Hell. The fascinating thing about this is they all quote the Bible to "prove" it, and there are many verses in the Scriptures that appear to support them. How can this be? Is the Bible not clear on the matter? Definitely, but, again, the error of many of the "Endurers" is not that they don't believe the verses, only that they misapply them. Remember, the Bible must be rightly divided to determine sound doctrine for a particular dispensation and this is where these groups fail. Otherwise, how could they "biblically" teach their doctrine? They don't imagine the verses, they are really there, and they do apply to somebody.

Though the Presbyterians and Baptists have always believed in the eternal security of a Christian, they both distort the matter. The former believe it for the wrong reasons and the latter force it to apply to every saved person in every dispensation. The Presbyterians believe one is secure because the believer was "predestinated" in eternity past to "persevere" (endure) in Christ until the end. They got this doctrine from their primary founder, John Calvin. It is the last point of their "five points of Calvinism" called "the perseverance of the saints." Many Baptists (though not all) realize all five points are nonsense and correctly believe a Christian is secure because he is **"preserved"** in Christ by God (Jude 1:1), not because he is "predestinated to persevere." Who when reading the Bible ever heard of such a thing as "perseverance of the saints"? God keeps the believer secure by sealing and preserving him in Christ (Eph. 4:30; 1 Thes. 5:23); it is not that the saint *must endure* because of predestination. Most Baptists believe in eternal security for the right reasons, but their tendency to force this preservation into every dispensation is just as serious an error as the Hyper-Calvinists.

When one begins to read the New Testament it is imperative he remember that the Bible is a Jewish book. The four gospels (especially Matthew) give account of a *Jewish Messiah* (Matt. 1), prophesied by

Jewish prophets (Isa. 53), who preaches repentance to Jews, so they could enter a *Jewish kingdom* (Matt. 4:17). Gentiles, as Gentiles, were out. Christ said Himself, **"I am not sent but unto the lost sheep of the house of Israel"** (Matt. 15:24), and also, **"salvation is of the Jews"** (John 4:22). His ministry was exclusively for Israel, thus, much of the first three gospels say little doctrinally to Gentiles. Of course, everything found in Matthew, Mark, and Luke is of benefit to Gentiles of today, but doctrinally much of the books are Jewish. The gospel of John has a much more doctrinal application to Gentiles because it was written well into the Church Age (@ 90 A.D), long after the doctrines of this dispensation were established. Matthew, on the other hand, is the most "Jewish" of the four. It was undoubtedly placed first in order in the New Testament because it is more like the Old Testament than any of the other three; more able to give the Bible a fluid transition from the Old Testament to the New. God knew what He was doing when He allowed the books to be placed in the order we have them in the *King James Version*. The order helps us understand God's entire program.

When studying the Bible every person must follow three essential guidelines for study to rightly divide the Scriptures. He must keep in mind WHO the passage was written to, who it APPLIES to, and does it doctrinally apply TODAY. If he just haphazardly gets his doctrine from here, there, and everywhere, he will at the least be confused and at the most teach deadly heresy. The author has found there are four books in the Bible that are the most abused by people who fail to properly divide the Scriptures. These books, thus abused, supply the "Bible" used by them to form most of the false doctrines floating around today. *Matthew, Acts, Hebrews,* and *Revelation* are the favorite books of every heretic in America; they are the biblical "ammunition" for his heresies. They don't realize all four of these books are transitional and deal with changing doctrines from one dispensation or testament to another.

In Matthew the transition is from the Old Testament books to the New; Acts details the gradual transition from Law to Grace; Hebrews is written to Hebrews concerning the transition from the old covenant to the new covenant with some application in the Tribulation; and Revelation shows the transition from Grace to the Tribulation, Tribulation to the Millennium, and finally from the Millennium to the New Heaven and Earth. What a group of books for one to get his doctrine from! These are four of the most difficult books in the Bible to unravel yet they are the favorites of those who today don't believe in eternal security or teach salvation by works. Failing to understand the transitional nature of these books and ignoring the plain, clear teaching of the epistles concerning the doctrines valid today, these people are a snare to themselves and to every one who hears them.

Since most of the events recorded in the four gospels took place under the Law, many details found in them won't match doctrines valid in the present Church Age as revealed in the epistles of Paul. For instance, one cannot find any **"Christians"** in any of the gospels because Christians are not mentioned until Acts 11:26. Before Acts 11 people were saved, but they were not Christians. We use the terms "Christian" and "saved" as synonymous today, but in the Bible saved people are not always Christians. Only those who have been regenerated and are in Christ are true Christians. Along with this no one in the gospels is said to be regenerated, in Christ, a part of the body of Christ, etc. until after the cross. Why? Because these blessings would not be available until after Christ's atonement, and they would not be fully revealed until years later.

Examining Matthew

Doctrines peculiar to the Jews and the Old Testament are common in Jesus' speech in the gospels. He preached, **"Repent for the kingdom of heaven is at hand"** (Matt. 4:17) to Israel because they were the only people promised such a kingdom and only to them was He sent. He went on to declare in the "Sermon on the Mount" the principles of this Jewish kingdom and the precepts that will be valid when it arrives. Let's look at some of these precepts and see how they compare to those given to the body of Christ.

The famous "beatitudes" declare certain blessings to those who are **"poor in spirit," "meek," "merciful," "pure in heart,"** who **"mourn,"** etc., without mentioning the gospel of the grace of God at all (1 Cor. 15:1-4). Where is the *death, burial,* and *resurrection* of Jesus Christ in the Beatitudes? Where is one told to have *faith in, believe on,* *or receive Christ for salvation?* **"Faith"** is only found once in the "sermon" (Matt. 6:30), and it deals with having faith in God to provide ones physical needs, not eternal salvation. It should be obvious to the most casual reader that the "Sermon on the Mount" does not have any gospel in it that is valid today. It contains a lot of good practical information, *but it is NOT the gospel for today.* The "sermon" deals exclusively with the gospel of the kingdom (Millennium).

Another example of the difference between these two gospels is Christ said in the "sermon" that if a person called another a fool he was in danger of **"hell fire"** (Matt. 5:22), yet Paul in the Church Age called the Galatians **"foolish"** (Gal. 3:1), is Paul in hell? Christ later even called people fools Himself, is He in danger? The Lord went on to say if a person in the kingdom cut off an offending member (eye, hand, etc.) it may help keep him out of hell (5:29-30). Will that help keep one out of hell today? Does not one today have to receive Jesus Christ to escape hell instead of mutilating himself? The "sermon" is filled with other works one must do during the kingdom to get or retain his salvation (5:41, 42, 46; 6:15, 20; 7:13, 24, 26; etc.), but what do they have to do with salvation today? Nothing.

Even though the "Sermon on the Mount" applies doctrinally in another dispensation, there are several passages in it that suit the Arminian's doctrine, and they constantly appeal to them for "proof." We have already mentioned one (Matt. 5:22), others are 5:44-45 where one has to do works to become and remain **"children of your father"** and 6:15 where one must forgive others before he can be forgiven. The implication, so the security deniers claim, is if one fails to forgive someone, God will not forgive him and the person will forfeit his salvation. Can a born again Christians lose his salvation if he fails to forgive someone? Nonsense, though somebody in another dispensation may not be forgiven for failing to forgive another, it is not a regenerated Christian. The difference is in the dispensations.

Further along in Matthew, in 8:11-12, one finds **"children of the kingdom"** being cast into **"outer darkness."** Does this have anything to do with someone in the body of Christ being cast into hell? Not in the least. The children cast out are the children of the *kingdom of heaven* (Mill.), not the *kingdom of God.* Here we must make a distinction between the **"kingdom of heaven"** and the **"kingdom of God."**

The kingdom of heaven is the *visible, physical, earthly, external, Jewish* kingdom promised to the descendants of Abraham through Jacob. The kingdom of God is the *invisible, immaterial, spiritual, internal* kingdom one is placed into when he is regenerated (Rom. 14:17). The kingdom of heaven is the *physical* side of God's promised kingdom, and the kingdom of God is the *spiritual.* Of course, Christ is the King of both, and both will be manifested when He returns. At the present time there can be *lost* people in the kingdom of heaven (tares, etc. Matt. 13), but none in the kingdom of God. Furthermore, people can be cast out of the kingdom of heaven but none can be cast out of the kingdom of God. The two kingdoms have little in common except Christ is the king of both. At the second advent the two kingdoms appear to, at least partially, merge together; but until then, one must keep them separate.

In Matthew chapter 12 the famous "unpardonable sin" is found; more fodder for the "Endurers." Does this passage say some today cannot be saved or that born again Christians can lose their salvation if they *"blaspheme the Holy Ghost"?* Not in the least. As with much of the rest of Matthew, this passage has doctrinal application to the Jews Christ said it to and will have further application to other Jews in the future. There are no Gentiles even hinted at in the passage, neither are any Christians mentioned (remember Acts 11:26?); the passage is purely Jewish. Moreover, Mark said the sin of blaspheming the Holy Spirit was *saying that Christ had an unclean spirit while He was on earth* (Mark 3:30). Christ is not physically on earth performing miracles and healings now, so how can one today blaspheme the Holy Spirit in the manner He was speaking of then? Many of the Pharisees may have at that time committed this sin by saying Christ **"hath"** an unclean spirit, but no one today has or can. Today one may resist the Holy Ghost and refuse to get saved, but this is not what Christ was referring to in Matthew chapter 12.

More Jewish kingdom of heaven doctrines can be found in Matthew chapter 13, and these can have some spiritual application today, but the chapters that supply most of the ammunition for the "Endurers" is chapters 24 and 25. In 24:13 Christ said **"he that shall endure to the end, the same shall be saved,"** but who is **"he"** and what or where is **"the end"**? Again, the **"he"** is not a Christian or even a Gentile, it is a Jew. Christ is speaking to Jews (notice how they are still keeping the Jewish sabbath vs. 20), His disciples are Jews, His nation is Jewish, and the kingdom He is proclaiming is Jewish. Born again Christians are foreigners in chapter 24. As for **"the end,"** is it the end of a person's life as the endurers claim? For the answer look at vs. 14. The gospel of the kingdom of heaven (not the gospel of the grace of God) will be preached (by Jews) throughout the world, **"then shall the end come."** The **"end"** is not the end of a person's life, it is the end of a period of time; *the Tribulation.*

The entire discourse of Christ found in chapters 24 and 25 is in response to the questions asked by His disciples in 24:3; **"when shall these thing be? and what shall be the sign of thy coming, and of the end of the world."** The whole passage applies after the (then un-known) Church Age, beginning with the Tribulation. If the Jews alive during the Tribulation endure to the end of it without taking the mark of the beast or being killed, and are also faithful to Christ and the proper works, they will be saved to enter into the Millennium. As with chapter 12, there are no Christians in the passage, neither are there any Gentiles; everything is Jewish.

Later in chapter 24 (vs. 48-51) one of Christ's servants is **"cut asunder"** and sentenced to weep and wail with the hypocrites in hell. Is this servant a Christian? Not on your life. He is an unregenerated, rebellious Jew meeting his Lord at the second advent. He did not "endure to the end" with clean hands or the right works and is consequently cast into hell.

Matthew 25:1-13 is a classic passage used by the "Endurers" and others to teach works are required for a Christian to keep his salva-tion. Here are some **"virgins"** who did not have enough oil to get into the wedding of their master and were barred entrance. They were cast out from the wedding. What does this have to do with a person getting saved today, though? Nothing. First of all the virgins were not the bride (Church) who marries the bridegroom (Christ), they were only there to meet Him. Second, Christ said to them **"I know you not"** (vs. 17); He couldn't say that to any Christian for He knows them all (John 10:27-28). Third, the virgins were to buy the oil (possibly the Holy Spirit) to enter into the supper. See how these kingdom of heaven parables are doctrinally inconsistent with the Church Age and the body of Christ? None of these Jewish virgins were regenerated, in Christ, sealed by the Holy Spirit, etc., they are Jews trying to get into the marriage supper of the Lamb as "friends" or "guests" at the end of the Tribulation. *The difference is in the dispensations.*

Later in chapter 25 another unprofitable servant is cast into **"outer darkness"** (vs. 29). Again, this is a kingdom of heaven parable and does not apply to believers who are in the kingdom of God. The unprofitable servant in Luke chapter 19 is in the kingdom of God and he does not go into outer darkness. He can't because *everyone* in the kingdom of God is regenerated and sealed by the Holy Spirit. In the last section of Matthew chapter 25, the judgment of the nations is described (vs 31-46), and it also is based entirely upon works. No faith, trust, or belief in anything is associated with this judgment; works are all that is considered. Those who have the right works are permitted into the kingdom (Millennium), and those who have the wrong works are cast out. The death, burial, and resurrection of Christ are not mentioned, and neither are the **"sheep"** said to be in Christ. Again, this passage has nothing to do with born again Christians. Though the **"sheep"** nations are Gentile nations, the passage has little to do with Gentiles nations today, and nothing to do with individual Gentiles being saved today. Have you had enough? We have only looked at some of the Jewish passages in Matthew, let alone the other gospels, and they don't match Gentile Church Age doctrines at all. Why the difference? *The difference is in the dispensations.*

The New Birth

We have been saying repeatedly all along that the new birth did not exist in the Old Testament and not even in the New until after the cross, and the reader may be wondering why. Another valid question that needs to be considered concerns when Christ told Nicodemus **"Ye must be born again"** (John 3:7). Surely Christ would not tell Nicodemus he needed something that was not yet available, would He? The answer is in John 3:6 and 7:39. In 3:6 Jesus said the new birth was a birth by the Holy Spirit, and in 7:39 the Holy Spirit clearly tells us through John, **"for the Holy Ghost was not yet given; because Jesus was not yet glorified."** The Holy Spirit was not given to anyone in the regeneration sense *until Christ was risen from death glorified* (John 14:16-17). Until the cross (really Pentecost) the Holy Spirit come upon and in people to empower them to do what God wanted them to do (Ex. 35:31), but He did not regenerate anyone. Christ's blood had to be shed to take the believer's sins away before the Holy Spirit would come in permanently to regenerate and seal him. His sins had to be redeemed and dealt with permanently (not just covered) before God would regenerate and indwell him permanently.

The Lord told Nicodemus **"ye must be born again"** because regeneration was required before anyone could enter **"the kingdom of God."** Even though the new birth was not yet available, Nicodemus should have known a spiritual rebirth was needed because every person's first birth from Adam was in sin. A **"master of Israel"** should realize man eventually needed a new nature before he could be in the kingdom of God and have the type of full relationship and fellowship with God, God desires. Even a saved person who has only his Adamic, fallen nature (like Abraham, Moses, David, etc.) is not equipped for the spiritual kingdom of God. This is the main reason none of the Old Testament saints went to heaven when they died. They were technically *still in their sins;* saved only by decree.

Only those who have had their spirit reborn unto righteousness, peace, and joy in the Holy Ghost (Rom. 14:17), and their sins *taken away* are prepared to enter the spiritual kingdom of God. Christ wasn't telling Nicodemus he could be born again at that time, only that it was a *prerequisite to entering the kingdom of God.* After Christ's death, resurrection, and glorification, the Holy Spirit was free to regenerate, and believers were then born again. In John 20:22 the risen Lord told His disciples **"receive ye the Holy Ghost,"** implying they would have Him in a different and fuller manner than before. Before the cross the disciples performed many miracles, healings, and exorcisms with the power of the Holy Spirit, but they could not receive him in the sense of regeneration until after the resurrection. From the resurrection to the rapture, every person who is saved is also born again and receives Christ's nature.

Even though many of the words found in the gospels were spoken to Jews under the Law and doctrinally only apply to them, that doesn't mean they are less important to believers in the Church

Age. Every word of God is precious and necessary for life (Matt. 4:4), and the passages that don't apply doctrinally today are still essential for the proper understanding of what God is doing. Likewise Paul said the things **"written aforetime were written for our learning"** (Rom. 14:4) and also for are **"admonition"** (1 Cor. 10:11). One must study the whole Bible, rightly dividing it, to have every truth God wants him to have. Whatever one finds in it that applies to him doctrinally, believe it, receive it, and act upon it. Whatever does not apply to him doctrinally, he should use it as an *example, admonition, instruction,* or *warning* to teach him more about God and His ways.

From Law To Grace

After the Jews rejected their Messiah's offer of the Kingdoms of Heaven and God and His terms for entering them, they with wicked hands delivered Him up as a criminal to death. The offers Jesus made concerning the kingdoms were legitimate, and if they would have received Him as a nation history would be much different. He would have set up His kingdom of heaven as promised (Matt. 3:17) and reigned as their King. His sacrificial death, of course, would still have to occur to permanently redeem believers, but it would have been under different circumstances. There is no use in speculating as to what would have happened if Israel had received Christ; they made their choice and did not receive Him (not then, anyway, Rom. 11). Nevertheless, Christ came to be their Messiah and would have began to fulfill all the promises God made to them then, but He was not the kind of king they expected or wanted, so they crucified Him.

Even though Israel as a nation refused Christ, around 500 individual Jews did believe on Him (1 Cor. 15:6) and soon became members of a new organism called the Church. The local church, which is simply a local assembly of believers, was first founded when Christ called out His disciples in Matthew chapter 10. The Church organism called the *Body of Christ*, however, did not began until the coming of the Holy Spirit on the day of Pentecost to regenerate, indwell, and seal believers. There is a obviously a distinct difference between the *local church* and the Church known as the **"Body of Christ."** Lost people (like Judas) can be members of a local church, but they cannot be part of the Body of Christ; it is only made up of regenerated Christians.

On the day of Pentecost around 120 disciples were gathered together when the Holy Ghost came to give them power (Acts 1:15, 2:1), but did the disciples know what all was happening to them? Not quite. They knew they were to receive power to evangelize the world (Acts 1:8) and also that the Holy Spirit was to be a **"comforter,"** but they by no means had a perfect understanding of what else was happening to them. The Bible student must remember that in Acts chapter 1 all that had been revealed to the disciples was the Old Testament embellished with the events of the past three and one-half years with Christ. They didn't yet have specific knowledge of the doctrines peculiar to the yet to be revealed Church. The first 15 chapters of Acts detail the transition from the well established doctrines of the Law to yet largely unknown doctrines of Grace.

Since the doctrines unique to Grace are so much different than the doctrines the Jews were used to, God gradually made the change-over over several years. That many Church Age doctrines were not yet revealed to the apostles on Pentecost doesn't mean they were not in effect at that time, though. The *new birth, salvation for Gentiles, the Body of Christ, etc.,* were valid from Pentecost onward, the disciples just didn't have complete knowledge of them. In the next section we will examine the major places in the book of Acts where the old doctrines were replaced by the new ones.

Unraveling Acts

Acts chapter 2 is one of the most abused chapters in the Bible. No less than four false belief systems are "founded" in this chapter. The modern proponents of *speaking in tongues, baptismal regeneration, Calvinistic predestination,* and *Hyper-dispensationalism* use this chapter to "prove" their doctrines. A chapter that gets this much attention is worthy of extra careful study. Relating to this the author has heard preachers (most of them Fundamentalists) speak of how Peter's sermon in chapter 2 is one of the greatest gospel sermons in history. Fine, *but what gospel?* Examine Acts 2 carefully and see if you find the gospel of the grace of God as revealed to Paul (1 Cor. 15:1-4) anywhere in it. Yes, the death, burial, and resurrection of Christ are mentioned, but what conclusions does Peter draw from these truths?

Does Peter mention **"ye must be born again?"** Does he mention that Christ died for anyone's sins (Paul said, Christ died four OUR sins)? Does he mention that individuals can personally receive Christ as their salvation? Does he even mention that people other than Jews can be saved at all? Furthermore, what did Peter tell the people to do after they said **"what shall we do"**? Does **"repent and be baptized..."** (2:38) match **"If thou shalt confess with thy mouth the Lord Jesus..."** (Rom. 10:9-10)? Not at all. Peter was telling the Jews as a group what to do in light of the fact they just crucified their Messiah, not how to be born again. As we said at that time there were several things Peter did not yet know about New Testament salvation. The message he preached was perfect for his time and audience, but it is by no means the standard for doctrine many make it today. In fact, Peter never preached Acts 2:38 again. He tried once, but the Holy Spirit wouldn't let him finish (ch.10)!

In Acts 2 Peter was simply trying to convince the Jews that the one they crucified was actually their God sent Messiah, hoping they would repent of their sin and receive Him. He began by quoting the prophet Joel (vs. 16) concerning the **"day of the Lord"** and the coming Tribulation (vs. 20) and stated **"whosoever shall call upon the name of the Lord"** will be saved from this terrible time. The coming of the Holy Spirit and the events that have just occurred (2:1-13) are not the fulfillment of the statements in vs. 17-21; this passage is a reference to the events immediately preceding Christ's return. Throughout the sermon Peter does not speak in terms of personal salvation, regeneration, justification, sanctification, etc. because these truths were still for the most part unknown. Salvation in the context is being saved from the negative effects of the **"Day of the Lord."**

Peter continues in chapter 2 by showing how Christ was **"approved of God"** being proven by the **"miracles and wonders and signs"** he performed (vs. 22), and also by His resurrection from the dead after they wickedly crucified Him (vs. 23-24). He goes on to quote David as proof that the Messiah could not remain dead but must be resurrected to reign on David's throne (vs. 31-32). Peter drives his point home by insisting the man they crucified has been declared by God as **"both Lord and Christ"** (vs. 36). This soul-piercing statement convicts the hearts of about 3000 of the **"house of Israel"** to the point that they ask **"what shall we do?"** Notice how the whole passage is unmistakingly Jewish. There is not a Gentile or uncircumcised person in sight. Peter's message is by a Jew, to Jews, about a rejected Jewish Messiah who came to set up a Jewish kingdom. It is eight chapters later before Peter is convinced that Gentiles can even be saved.

What Peter told the Israelites to do after they were pricked in their heart with guilt also shows Pentecost was a unique situation. Contrary to what many claim today, Acts 2:38 is not the gospel or the means of salvation today. It is simply what Peter told the them to do after realizing they crucified their Messiah. Again, no personal guilt is mentioned; no regeneration, justification, sanctification, or eternal redemption is mentioned; no personal indwelling Savior is mentioned, he just tells them to **"repent and be baptized..."** (because God had already forgiven them [Luke 23:34]) so they could receive the Holy Ghost. Does this sound like John 1:12-13, 3:16, 5:24; Romans 4:5, 10:9-10; etc?

The Jews in Acts 2 had to be baptized before they could receive the Holy Spirit according to Peter. Do we have to be baptized in water to receive Him today? That these events occur in the same dispensation we are in today doesn't change things. Peter couldn't tell the people what he didn't know. God had forgiven Israel for crucifying their Messiah and gave them another chance to receive Him as such, and those who were willing to had to be baptized in Jesus' name to show their repentance. As a result God would give them the promised Holy Spirit. Only 3000 accepted the offer, though; Israel as a nation did not repent.

See the difference between salvation as found in Acts chapter 2 and how it is described in Romans, Galatians, Ephesians, and even later in Acts? Acts 2 details a transitional period from Law to Grace and the salvation doctrines found in it (that one must be baptized to receive the Holy Spirit [vs. 38], etc.) do not apply to anybody today. As we said they didn't even apply to anybody after Pentecost. Again, salvation as described in Romans, Galatians, Ephesians, etc. was valid in Acts 2, however, *nobody but God knew it.* He revealed it in His own good time. Salvation as we know it now did not become finalized in Acts until *chapter 15,* so anyone who uses chapter 2 as the foundation of their doctrine is appealing to a transitory situation that has long since passed away.

In Acts 3:12-26 Peter preached another sermon to Israel with much the same tone as the former. He again declares how they crucified the **"Prince of Life"** (vs. 15) and proves He is yet alive by the healing of the lame man (vs. 16). Peter admits they crucified Christ in ignorance, but still insists they must repent to be converted back to God. If they will repent as a nation and accept Christ, Peter tells them, God will quickly send Christ back to be their King and bring with Him their promised kingdom. But, again, Israel refused. See how the first few chapters of Acts deal only with Jewish matters and not with Church doctrines that were revealed later? The difference this time is not in the dispensations, but in how the dispensations are perceived. Peter is behaving as though he is still under the Law. A new dispensation has arrived, but by no fault of his own he just doesn't know much about it. Likewise, those who received Peter's messages in chapters 2 and 3 were regenerated and justified exactly like believers today, they just didn't know much about the specifics of salvation either.

God gave Israel and Jerusalem one more chance to repent and receive their Messiah with the message Stephen delivered in Acts 7, but they again refused and this time killed the messenger. After this violent rejection God quit dealing exclusively with the Jews and began to openly offer salvation to others. In Acts chapter 8 there are two interesting, but different, salvation situations. In the first part of the chapter, Philip went down to Samaria and preached Christ to them, performing miracles to back up his words, and the Samaratians listened to him (vs. 5-8). As a result some of them believed his words about Christ and agreed to be baptized (vs. 12). *Were they saved?* According to vs. 16 the Holy Spirit had not come on any of them. Can one be saved and not be indwelt with the Holy Spirit (John 3:6)? In chapter 2 the believing Jews received the Holy Spirit when they were baptized, these Samaratians, however, did not.

From the *New Testament* perspective these people were not saved until they received the Holy Spirit (vs. 17), but in the Old Testament sense they could have been saved in vs. 12. See the transition? The half-breed Gentiles baptized in vs. 12 were not truly saved because they are in the *Dispensation of Grace* where one must be born again by the Holy Spirit to enter the kingdom of God. Hypothetically, if they would have believed on Christ before the cross under the *Dispensation of the Law*, they very well may have been saved! Saved only on a "trial basis" "on credit," though (see chapter 2). God is showing the apostles, disciples, Samaratians, and us today his further transition into Church Age doctrines. After Israel's vehement rejection of Him in chapter 8, God began leading His servants to preach to other groups, beginning with the half-breed Samaratians.

Later in chapter 8 Philip is instructed to go south, and when he did he found an Ethiopian eunuch reading from Isaiah 53. God had prepared this eunuch's heart, and when Philip got to him he was ripe for the picking. All Philip had to do was explain to him the suffering person in Isaiah was Jesus Christ suffering as a substitute for others, The Ethiopian received his words gladly. Here, the gospel of the grace of God is beginning to take its present form. This is the first account in the Bible of an *individual* personally receiving Jesus Christ for his salvation with *no works or baptism involved.* Verse 37 (not found in most of the corrupt "new Bibles") is clear that the eunuch based his salvation on belief in Christ. Philip wanted to be sure of the sincerity of his profession before he baptized him. Salvation is looking more like Romans with every chapter we progress in Acts, and in chapter 9 God saves the man who wrote Romans. Instead of Christianity being a "Jewish sect," it is becoming more and more Gentile the farther we go. In chapter 2 only Jews were saved; in chapter 8 some "half-breed" Jews were saved and a Gentile proselyte to Judaism. Only full blooded non proselyte Gentiles are left to be saved, and God does this in Chapter 10.

Cornelius

At first glance one may think the Gentile, Cornelius, was a saved man. He was devout, feared God, gave much alms to people, was a man of constant prayer, and received visions from God. But the Holy Spirit tells us during all this he was *dead lost* (Acts 11:14). God even said his prayers and alms came up before Him as *a memorial* (so much for those who insist God doesn't hear the prayers of lost people) while he was still *dead in trespasses and sins!* Cornelius is a perfect picture of the man described in Romans 2:6-16 who follows his conscience towards God and His truth. Cornelius knew there was a God and that he himself was a sinner, and he knew he needed to make peace somehow with this God before he would be accepted by Him. Therefore, Cornelius lived right, prayed, gave alms, and instructed his house to do likewise; this is all he knew to do. God, however, is ready to reveal to Him (and Peter) some new truths that can release Cornelius and all other Gentiles from their sins.

The Lord told Cornelius to send men to Joppa to get a certain man (vs. 5), and he will tell him what more he needs to do (vs. 6). Though they were ready to receive and hear the man who spoke for God, Peter wasn't quite ready to oblige them. He still thought Gentiles were unclean and unacceptable for salvation. This is one of the strongest proofs that Acts is a transitional book and the early chapters are not fixed doctrine for the Church Age. Regardless of how some may "interpret" Matthew 28:19-20; Acts 1:8; and Acts 2:39, Peter and the rest of the apostles thought salvation was only available to Jews. God had to put Peter in a trance and show him a vision *three times* to convince him Gentiles have been **"cleansed"** (vs. 15) and the wall between them and salvation had been broken down. They could now be saved without becoming Jews (proselytes). By the time the men from Cornelius arrive, Peter is fully convinced of this and goes back with them entering Cornelius' house with a clear conscience.

After hearing what God told Cornelius to do, Peter begins his message. He again states he is now persuaded **"God is no respecter of persons"** and any person in any nation who fears Him and works righteousness is accepted for the opportunity of salvation (vs. 35). **"Accepted with Him"** is not salvation itself, but one being accepted in the sense that he is given the opportunity to be saved. Peter learned a great lesson that day. Doctrinally, Gentiles could have been saved ever since Pentecost, but no one knew it until God revealed it to Peter. After explaining this Peter continues his message and begins to preach **"Jesus."** He states (similar as he did in chapter 2) how Jesus was anointed by God with the Holy Ghost (vs. 38), how He healed people, and how He was slain and hanged on a tree by His own people as a criminal (vs. 38). Peter then boldly proclaims how God raised Christ from the dead and showed Him openly to witnesses, him being one (vs. 40-41), and further testifies that Jesus is ordained of God to be the Judge of all men, living and dead (vs. 42). Peter doesn't confront these Gentiles for the act of crucifying their Messiah as he did the Jews, he simply tells them **"Jesus of Nazareth"** is the Judge of all mankind and will judge every man according to His righteousness. After this Peter tells them in vs. 43 that through this once dead but now living Judge's name **"whosoever believeth in Him shall receive remission of sins."** This statement was what Cornelius and his house was waiting to hear. When they learned salvation was in Jesus Christ, they immediately believed on Him and were saved (vs. 44-45).

The quick salvation of the Gentiles came as a surprise to Peter because he had not finished his message or given any type of invitation. He was likely going to finish as he did in chapter 2 with **"Repent and be baptized..."** or something similar, but God prevented his plans and saved them; giving them the Holy Spirit, through their faith alone. After Peter sees the Holy Ghost come upon them and hears them speak with other tongues as the Jews did at Pentecost, he instructs them to be baptized in water. This is believer's baptism: *baptism after one is saved.* In chapter 2 the Jews had to be baptized to get the Holy Spirit, but not any more. The method of salvation has changed. God has now revealed He will save believers *through faith apart from any works,* including baptism, and their salvation is just as valid as that of the Jews (vs. 47). Now salvation is no longer exclusively Jewish. Gentiles have now been accepted as they are for salvation, and they will multiply rapidly.

Though Peter's message was similar to the one in chapter 2, it was also tailored for his Gentile audience. Along with not calling Jesus their Messiah (Christ is the Messiah only to Israel), he tells them they must believe in Him before they receive remission of sins. He told Israel they must repent and be baptized **"for"** (because of) the past remission of sins. Also in chapter 2 Peter addressed Israel collectively as a nation concerning national repentance, here his message is to individuals and deals with personal faith. Since the Jews have rejected Christ over and over, God is moving to the Gentiles, and they are receiving Him. Since salvation has become "Gentile," the doctrines of salvation as they are today are quickly becoming established.

In chapter 13 Paul preaches Peter's Gentile faith gospel to some Jews (Paul learned this gospel directly from God, not through Peter, Gal. 1:12) and ended by saying, **"And by Him all that believe are justified from all things from which ye could not be justified from the law of Moses"** (vs. 39). Salvation is now clearly based upon faith in Jesus Christ's finished work on the cross. This faith will avail a person, Jew or Gentile, of the justification he could not receive regardless of the amount of works he performed under the Law of Moses. Faith alone; purely by faith; **"By grace are ye saved, through faith."**

The Disciples Meet

Even though Peter, Paul, and a few others understood salvation was now only through faith apart from works, many other Jews were not yet convinced and a meeting was held in Jerusalem to settle the issue. Acts chapter 15 give the details of this meeting and is therefore *the most important chapter in Acts dealing with salvation.* Not chapter 2, chapter 8, or even chapter 10, but chapter 15. This chapter is so important because it finalizes and settles the matter of how salvation is obtained by every believer everywhere until the rapture. Those who teach salvation by works or baptismal regeneration have to ignore this chapter because it supersedes the "Bible" they use to teach their heresies.

There were two questions under consideration at this meeting. One was a person must do something (be circumcised and keep the Law of Moses) to BE saved (vs. 1); the other was one must do something (good works, etc.) to STAY saved (vs.4). The old Jewish ways die hard. The apostles gathered together to discuss these issues, and after much disputing Peter stood up among them and settled the questions. He did so by reminding them of how God used him to preach the gospel to the Gentiles and how God, by considering their hearts, not their works, gave them the Holy Spirit when they believed. By doing this God put no difference between Jews and Gentiles, purifying the hearts of both by faith (vs. 8-9). Peter goes on to rebuke his Jewish brethren for attempting to burden the believing Gentiles with the yoke of the Law, which they themselves could not bear (vs. 10). He concludes his words by saying Jews will NOW be saved as Gentiles are saved (vs. 11)! Amazing! Salvation is no longer by the Jewish method of Acts 2:38 but by the Gentile methods revealed in chapter 10 and later! For the first time since the days of Abraham, salvation is Gentile instead of exclusively Jewish. Peter spells it out when he says **"we** (Jews) **shall be saved even as they"** (Gentiles) indicating the change (vs. 11).

Again, God has through 15 chapters of transition finalized and established His method of salvation during this dispensation and it has a definite Gentile ring to it. Jews can, of course, still be saved, but they must be saved just like Gentiles are by trusting Christ as their sole redemption. Gentiles are the wild olive branch grafted into the root of God's salvation tree until the natural branches, the Jews, are grafted back in after the fullness of the Gentiles comes in (Rom. 11:17-27).

Chapter IV
Salvation In The New Testament cont.

Since in the book of Acts salvation became predominately Gentile, it is only logical the following books of the Bible (Romans—Philemon) apply doctrinally to the Gentile Church. Most of the three epistles of John also apply to this age as well as much of the epistles of Peter. We know this because the books are addressed to either New Testament churches (Rom. — 2 Thes.), to individual ministers (1 Tim.—Tit.), or to other Christians. The books *Hebrews* and *James*, however, are not written to born again Christians but to Jews. Hebrews means Hebrews, not Gentiles, and James is addressed to the **"twelve tribes"** (Jam. 1:1), not the body of Christ. Remember, knowing who a book or epistle is written to is imperative for sound Bible study.

Paul's epistle to the Romans is clearly a Gentile, church age book, and because of its emphasis on doctrine, it is often called "the Constitution of the Christian faith." The Holy Spirit caused this book to be placed immediately after Acts even though it was written later than most of Paul's other books because He wanted the Bible reader to be grounded in sound Christian doctrine. In the first eight chapters, Paul explains how salvation is by faith alone apart from any works (4:5) and then defines salvation's exceedingly rich blessings with terms *like justification, propitiation, adoption, imputation, redemption, reconciliation, sanctification, etc.* These are all doctrines that apply to every Christian NOW, not to blessings he will receive in the future. Romans should be studied by the believer until he knows its rich doctrines by heart; only then can he begin to appreciate what God has done for him.

How Many Gospels?

The rest of the epistles of Paul following Romans further explain New Testament salvation and reveal other truths essential to Christian doctrine; every Christian has a responsibility to study these also. The truths found in these books make up what is called **"my gospel"** by Paul. This gospel is the gospel of the grace of God with the added doctrines revealed only to Paul. It is one of the *four different gospels* found in the Scriptures. The author has heard prominent ministers proclaim with certainty, "There is only one gospel from Genesis 1 to Revelation 22, and it is the gospel of Jesus Christ..." They imply with these words anyone who believes otherwise is in error and not true to the Bible. But what does the Bible say? Anyone who tries to study the Scriptures objectively will soon see it contains more than one gospel. There is the **"gospel of the kingdom"** found in Christ's ministry; the **"gospel of the grace of God"** valid during this age; Paul's **"my gospel,"** mentioned above; and the **"everlasting gospel."** These gospels are all different and anyone who makes them the same has to forcefully wrest the Scriptures to do it.

The **"gospel of the kingdom"** of Heaven (Matt. 4:23) Christ preached was the good news that the kingdom promised to Abraham and David was nigh and ready to be entered when the King was received. It had nothing to do with the new birth or individual salvation, it dealt with a physical, visible, literal kingdom. This gospel has been replaced with the **"gospel of the grace of God"** for the time being but will again be preached to the Jews during the Tribulation before Christ's return.

The *"Gospel of the Grace of God"* (1 Cor.15:1-4) is the familiar gospel of today and speaks of the suffering, death, burial, and resurrection of the Lord Jesus Christ. It declares how He suffered and died for man's sins and rose from the dead to supply His salvation to all who will receive Him.

Again, Paul's **"my gospel"** (2 Tim. 2:8) is simply this gospel with added revelations concerning the *Body of Christ, the Church, the mysteries, etc.* Even though Paul's gospel includes the Gospel of the Grace of God, the two are not identical. The former includes the latter, but one only needs to receive the latter to be saved.

The **"everlasting gospel"** (Rev. 14:6) is a gospel that does not even mention Christ. It is a message of repentance to Gentiles beginning with the Tribulation and continuing on into eternity. It in no way resembles the other gospels in content or doctrine, destroying the idea there is only one. All the **"everlasting gospel"** says is man is to *fear, worship, and give glory to God* because He is about to Judge somebody.

It says nothing about Christ's substitutionary death even though it is called **"everlasting."** Interesting.

The Holy Spirit has shown us there is a difference between the gospels in Galatians 1. In verse 8 Paul says, **"though we or an angel from heaven preach any other gospel unto you than that we have preached unto you, let him be accursed."** In Revelation 14:6, however, we find an angel preaching another gospel and he is not accursed. *The difference is in the dispensations.* The **"everlasting gospel"** is cursed in this age and Paul's gospel will be out of place in the Tribulation. Even the **"gospel of the kingdom"** is cursed in this age because it does not match the gospel Paul preached.

Understanding Hebrews

With the book of Hebrews, the Bible begins to take on a Jewish twist again. With the thirteen books preceding it dealing with the Body of Christ, the Holy Spirit now begins to again address the Jews. As the title of the book is *Hebrews,* why would anyone think it applied doctrinally to Gentile Christians? Of course, there is much in the book a Christian can learn and profit from, but if he tries to apply it all doctrinally to the Church Age he will soon run into "contradictions." The writer of Hebrews is trying to convince both lost and saved Hebrews that the new covenant established by Christ's death is superior to the old covenant of the Law. The temptation of saved Hebrews backsliding back into the bondage of the Law is very great, and Paul wants to strengthen the hearers of this book in what Christ's redemption has done for them.

The thought that Hebrews was written to both lost and saved people should not be strange to the reader, Paul addressed parts of other letters to lost people also (1 Cor. 15:4, etc.). The emphasis of Hebrews appears to apply to Hebrews in the Tribulation when Israel is again the main object of God's dealings. This is why the believers who believe a Christian can lose his salvation appeal to Hebrews as their "proof." There are passages in the book that do indicate someone can fall from salvation, but as we will see, they do not refer to a regenerated Christian.

Hebrews 3:6 and 14 is the first place the "Endurers" stop, but look at the whole passage. Verse 6 says **"whose house are we IF we hold fast...unto the end."** The **"if"** is the word pointed to by these people, "What **"if"** you don't hold out to the end" they say. First of all, do you find any reference to a blood washed, regenerated, Holy Spirit sealed Christian in the passage? Also, what is **"the end"** in both verses referring to? What makes you think it is the end of a person's life after reading Matthew 24:13-14? The **"end"** is the end of a period of time just like in Matthew 24:14. The **"rest"** in Heb. chapter 2 shows this to be true by illustrating how the Israelites in the wilderness had to endure in faith to the end of their wanderings before they could enter into God's rest—Canaan land (vs. 7-19). The **"we"** throughout the passage refers not to Christians but to Hebrews; "...**whose house are we** (Hebrews) **if we** (Hebrews) **hold fast unto the end"** (vs. 6); **"for we** (Hebrews) **are made partakers of Christ if we** (Hebrews) **hold...unto the end"** (vs. 14). See how keeping in mind who a book is written to clears things up? There is no reference to a born again Christian anywhere in the passage, neither is there any mention of anyone going to hell. The passage applies doctrinally to Hebrews in the Tribulation period enduring to the end of it in faith so they can enter into the promised land (Millennium) and partake of Christ. Don't allow those who refuse to rightly divide the Scriptures misapply them and talk you out of your security in Christ. *Hebrews deals with Hebrews.*

The next controversial passage is in chapter 6, and here the "Security-deniers" have a field day. The **passage "For it is impossible...if they fall away to renew them again unto repentance..."** (vs. 4-6) is often quoted by the "Arminians," but they have bitten of more than they can chew. The passage clearly says it is **"impossible"** to renew again those who fall away, but all the Endurers claim one can be saved again after he falls away. These verses also give fits to many Baptists, who correctly believe a Christian cannot lose his salvation, but cannot understand the verses as they stand. They come up with all kinds of "interpretations" to force the verses to conform to their doctrine. Some Fundamentalists insist the passage is "hypothetical," but the text doesn't even hint this. Others claim it refers to people like the spies at Kadesh-Barnea (Num. 13-14) who were not saved but on the threshold of salvation. However, verse 4 says those who can fall tasted of the **"heavenly gift"** and partook of the **"Holy Ghost."** To **"taste"** something means to have it, just like Christ tasted death for every man (Heb. 2:9). This one passage has those on both sides of the eternal security issue squirming to appear "scholarly" and save face.

Obviously, someone in Hebrews 6:1-4 is in danger of losing his salvation, but again, it is not a born again Christian. Did you notice in verses 1-2 where the writer refers to the principles of the doctrines of Christ (*repentance, faith, baptisms, laying on of hands, resurrection of the dead, and eternal judgment*), that he does not mention ONE doctrine unique to salvation in the Church Age? *Regeneration, the new nature, the Body of Christ, the sealing of the Holy Spirit, justification, imputation, etc.,* are not mentioned. How can one explain this? Simple, the writer is not referring to a regenerated Christian. He is again referring to Hebrews in another dispensational setup.

It is very likely Hebrews (at least the first 12 chapters) was written early in the book of Acts (probably before chapter 12; certainly before chapter 15) when no one knew much at all about a new birth or that a new, non Hebrew, dispensation was made possible at the cross. This explains a lot. The writer didn't mention Church Age doctrines because he didn't know of such things. He may have not even yet known Gentiles could be saved. Therefore, anybody who uses Hebrews to teach Gentile Church Age doctrine is ignorant of God's dispensational arrangments. At the time it was written, Hebrews applied to Jews who believed Christ was the Messiah before the Church Age doctrines were fully known and established in Acts 15. However, now, Hebrews speaks directly to Hebrews who will be alive during the Tribulation after the Church is gone. Remember, the Bible speaks to people of all ages; it is not limited to Fundamentalists in the Church Age.

If there is any doubt that Hebrews applies doctrinally in the Tribulation look at verse 11. There we find the characteristic **"the end"** again—the end of the Tribulation. When one realizes this the passage easily falls into place. The **"those"** in vs. 4 are saved people in the Tribulation sense, not the Church Age sense. If the saved person falls away in the Tribulation (takes the mark of the Beast, for instance), he forfeits his salvation and cannot get it back (Rev. 14:9-12)! Furthermore, if the Church goes through the Tribulation as many today claim, then a Christian *must in some way be able to lose his salvation or else the Scriptures contradict!* Thank God Christ's bride will not suffer this wrath (1 Thess. 1:10).

This passage in Hebrews fits perfectly with the other passages we have looked at concerning salvation after the Church Age (Matt. 5-7, 24-25; Heb. 3). The Hebrews that will be saved then will be decreed saved like those in the Old Testament. Each individual is in danger of losing his salvation if he doesn't do the right works or fails to endure to the end (vs. 11). If (remember **"if"** in Hebrews chapter 3?) he endures and does make it, he will become a partaker of Christ (3:14). The **"powers of the world to come"** (Mill.) will be the signs and wonders performed by the "two witnesses" and others during the Tribulation (Rev. 11). All the passages coincide. The writer of Hebrews says in 6:9 he is persuaded of better things of those who he wrote to at the time (around 35-40 A.D.), but the reason he says this is because of their works (vs. 10-11)! Works play an important part in the Tribulation, and we will deal more with salvation during that time shortly.

The third passage in Hebrews the Arminians and others use to prove a Christian can fall out of Christ and go to hell is in chapter 10. This passage gets heavy use by the "Endurers" because of the way it is worded, **"For if we sin wilfully after that we have received knowledge of the truth there remaineth no more sacrifice for sins, But a fearful looking for of judgment and fiery indignation which shall devour the adversaries."** The Endurers point to this passage and glibly say, "See there? If a Christian sins willfully after he is saved he can lose his salvation and go to Hell!" Really? Are there any Born again Christians found anywhere in the passage? Is there any hint of a Spirit sealed believer being *plucked out of Christ, unborn again, forsaken by Christ and God, severed from the Body of Christ, etc., and cast into the Lake of Fire?* Nonsense. You couldn't find a regenerated Christian in the passage with a microscope. True, someone in the passage can lose his salvation, but, again, it is not anyone in the Body of Christ.

Though the Arminians wrest this passage to teach their saved-today, lost-tomorrow theology, the Fundamentalists fare little better.

They either won't allow the person who sins to be a true believer but only one who had **"knowledge"** of the truth, or they "Greekify" the verses and force them to conform to Church Age doctrine. Concerning their first argument, verse 7 says the fallen man was **"sanctified"** by the blood of Christ. This speaks of more than just a head knowledge of Christ, the man was sanctified by Him. This is knowledge in the sense of experience.

Concerning the "Going to the original Greek" method of dealing with this passage, many will contend a Christian will not willfully sin habitually and appeal to the tense of some Greek word to "prove" it. But the passage says nothing about one habitually continuing in sin; it plainly says if one sins **"wilfully"**! *One sin can be enough.* (When the English Bible God has used for nearly 400 years (AV 1611) won't support these "scholars," they immediately run to the "Greek" to change it and usually distort the text so much they themselves can't make sense of it after they change it!)

Even though the text says nothing about someone sinning habitually, to say a Christian *cannot willfully sin habitually is absurd;* millions do it all the time. To say different is to deny a Christian his *free will* and pretend his old, Adamic nature is powerless. Every Christian is just as capable of sinning as a lost man because he still has the *old nature* of a dead, lost man in him! This fallen nature is not eradicated at conversion. True, every believer also has the new, righteous nature of Christ in him, but the old is still there to tug and pull for its own way. Because of his new nature, no Christian HAS TO sin at anytime, but he is always capable of sin until death or the rapture.

In general, Christians as a whole usually don't sin openly as much as lost people, however, sometimes they do, and some in an backslidden state will habitually sin more (visibly) than some lost people. Though every lost person is dead in sin and can only sin, the rebellious believer may do things a "moral" lost person deems immoral and would never do! Every believer should realize, however, open sin is just the outward manifestation of sin that has already occurred in the heart. A person's heart can harbor and entertain sin whether the sin is outwardly seen or not. Who can forget the words of Christ in Matthew chapter 5 where he brands the lustful person an *adulterer* and also 1 John 3:15 where the Holy Spirit calls the hater *a murderer?* Sins don't have to be outward to be sin; the secret sins *of envy, jealously, pride, selfishness, greed, lust, hate, resentment, contempt, self-pity, self-will, worry, not content, etc.,* are sins all Christians entertain willingly to some degree and many habitually! All one has to do is talk to a few to find this out. Nevertheless, even with these wicked and vile sins, no Christian can lose his salvation. *The difference is in the dispensations.*

Now, since this passage doesn't doctrinally refer to Christians in the Church Age, where does it apply? Again, in the Tribulation period. This is clear from the Old Testament quotations found in verse 30 (Deut. 32:30-36) referring to the song of Moses sang after the exodus and in the Tribulation (Rev. 15:3). You didn't check the cross-references did you? Blindly following to interpretation of your favorite "scholar" and failing to personally compare Scripture with Scripture will lead to a **"private interpretation"** more times than not. Also, the mention of **"his people"** in a book called Hebrews should indicate to the most jaded eyes that the passage applies distinctly to Hebrews. The passage is clearly Jewish and can only deal with Jews in the Tribulation. Since there is no new birth in the Tribulation to regenerate and seal believers, a person then can be on the *right path, taste of the heavenly gift, believe in Christ, be sanctified by the Christ's blood, have good works, etc.,* in essence be saved as much as anyone then can be and then **"sin willfully"** and loose all he had. Whether he denies Christ and His blood atonement, takes the mark of the Beast, or fails to continue in the required works (Matt. 25), he has *fallen from his salvation.* During this period people likely will be initially saved by faith alone, but each must continue in the right works and keep the commandments of God to stay saved. If one sins willfully in an area that can cost him his salvation, he has had it.

Verse 31 says **"it is a fearful thing to fall into the hands of the living God,"** and it will be for the Hebrews who fall away in the Tribulation, but it is not fearful for a Christian. Every Christian is IN God's hand permanently, and no one can take him out (John 10)! Furthermore, every born again believer is a part of Christ's Body, and thus also a part of or connected to His hand! What speaks of terror and judgment to a rebellious Hebrew in the Tribulation speaks of peace and security to a believer in Christ. Again, the difference is in the dispensations.

The book of Hebrews loses much of its difficulty when one rightly divides it and does not force the distinctly Jewish passages to apply to a period where they do not belong. As we mentioned forcing these passages to doctrinally apply in the Church Age will either lead one to believe a Christian can lose his salvation or cause him to wrest them by his **"private interpretation"** to make them line up with his doctrine. Either way the Scriptures are misused. The "Endurers" are at least *honest* in trying to take the verses at face value, they just apply them to the wrong people. The Fundamentalists, however, refuse to take them as they stand, showing their infidelity, and change their obvious meaning by appealing to "the Greek" and "scholarship." The verses as they stand simply give them fits. Nevertheless, for one reason or another many of them will cling to their shallow and inconsistent "historical positions" rather than yield to the plain words of the Scriptures. Unfortunately, the ethics of many Fundamentalists in their treatment of the Scriptures is often inferior to their Arminian counterparts.

James

Like Hebrews, the book of James is another epistle that is not addressed to Gentile believers in the Church Age. James 1:1 says, **"to the twelve tribes scattered abroad"** clearly stating this book is also written to Hebrews. As with the other Jewish passages, there is much one can learn in James, but he must remember doctrinally it is Jewish. This explains why in chapter 2 works are connected with saving faith. The last 13 verses of chapter 2 have been used by people for centuries to "prove" works are required before one can become a true Christian, and many genuine Christians also use the same passage to prove one must work to remain a Christian. What is interesting is the verses seem to support them, **"though a man say he hath faith, and have not works? can faith save him?"** (vs. 14); **"that faith without works is dead"** (vs. 20); **"ye see then how that by works a man is justified, and not by faith only"** (vs. 24); etc. But do these verses apply to Christians in the Church Age? Surely you know the answer by now.

They doctrinally apply to Hebrews with full application during the Tribulation.

Needless to say, there is no contradiction between the theology of James and Paul even though it may appear so to those who refuse to study. Paul says no less than five times that works are in no way connected with a person receiving salvation (Rom. 3:20, 4:5; Gal. 2:16; Eph. 2:8-9; Tit. 3:5; etc.) and James says in his book they are. *The difference, again, is in the dispensations.* See, again, how important it is to understand who wrote a book, who it is written to, and who it applies to when studying the Bible? Without constantly keeping these essentials in mind sound doctrine will bypass you. If Hebrews and James do fully apply to believers in the Church Age then the Bible would contradict! But the Holy Spirit has removed all contradiction and much exegetical difficulty by showing us these books apply to Jews and for the most part in another dispensation. Like Hebrews, James was likely written early in the book of Acts before the Church Age doctrines were fully revealed and understood. It may have been written by the original apostle James before he was murdered in Acts 12. This would easily explain its Jewish message from an historical standpoint.

Salvation in the Tribulation

When the rapture occurs and Christ takes His Church into Heaven with Him, things will never be the same on earth again. When all those in Christ are raised up to meet their Savior in the air, a whole dispensational system will go up with them. Eternal salvation as we know it today (by grace through faith apart from works) will no longer be valid because the Holy Spirit will no longer regenerate and seal those who become saved after the **"trump"** (1 Thes. 4:16). Believers in the future will not have a new nature, be placed in Christ, or have Christ permanently indwelling them. Simply put, the means of salvation as we know it today will *no longer exist.* The difference in the dispensations will make it impossible for a believer to be born again, placed into Christ's Body, or keep eternal life by faith alone. Salvation will be *very similar* to the way it was in the Old Testament.

In light of this, consider how thankful and grateful we who are saved today should be. Many of the blessings God bestows upon the Church today are blessings He bestows upon no other group at any other time. How gracious and generous God is to us. It seems He picked the Church to show all creation just how kind gracious, and loving He can be. He not only took our sins and died for them in our place, He by the *NEW BIRTH placed every believer into His family and gave each His own eternal life and very nature!* He did not do this for Abraham, Moses, or David. It is all by grace, pure grace. How much more we should love, praise, and serve Him.

When the rapture occurs the number of people making up the Body of Christ will be complete and fixed. No one then or now can possibly fall out of the body, and no one in the future can enter it. When the voice of the archangel is heard, the door to the Church will be forever sealed.

Contrary to the theology of many of today's prophetic preachers, nowhere in the Bible does it say that the Tribulation will begin immediately after the rapture. It very well may, but it doesn't have to. Nevertheless, whether immediately or months or years later, the Tribulation will began with the Antichrist signing a seven year covenant with Israel. As we mentioned earlier after the rapture Israel again becomes the main object of God's dealings with man and salvation will again have a Jewish ring to it.

The Tribulation will be a very difficult time for one to try and live for God. Christ declared in Matthew 24 this period will contain *terror, horror,* and *death* on a scale the world has not yet seen. One reading of the book of Revelation with all the catastrophes, judgments, and sorrows found in it should awaken any believing reader to the shear horror many will endure during this period. As we have repeatedly said, during this seven year period faith alone will not be enough to permanently secure ones eternal salvation. Faith will likely be the means of the believer initially being saved, but his faith must motivate the proper works for him to keep his salvation, and he must be faithful in keeping them to **"endure to the end."** Remember how James said, **"Faith without works is dead,"** and one shows his faith by working? In the Tribulation one must show his faith and work to overcome evil and clinging to good or else he won't make it through saved (Rev. 3:5). There are around 200 verses in the New Testament that indicate someone can lose his salvation—they must fit somewhere—and the Tribulation is the place. Remember Matthew chapters 24 and 25, and Hebrews chapters 3, 6, and 10? The Tribulation is where they all doctrinally apply: the **"time of Jacob's trouble"** (not the Church's trouble). Again, someone in the Bible can lose his salvation, but it is not a born again Christian.

During the Tribulation salvation will be identical to salvation under the law as far as what happens to and inside a believer is concerned. Since there is no longer a new birth available, nothing will happen inside the believer to secure his salvation. Though he won't be saved on credit as those in the Old Testament were (because Christ's atonement has since been made), he will still be saved on a trial basis like they were. Believing on Christ will just be the *first step* in his process of salvation, for along with believing he must **"keep the commandments of God"** (Rev. 12:17, 14:12, 22:14, CHECK THESE!). Since this is, again, a Jewish dispensation, the commandments must be the Ten Commandments and other commandments given under the law. Gentiles will likely not be obligated to keep the distinctly Jewish commandments, but they must keep the moral commandments as much as they know them even if their conscience is their only guide.

The quickest way for anyone in the Tribulation to forfeit his salvation is to take the *mark of the Beast.* Anyone who takes that mark is doomed without any hope of future salvation (14:9-11). One in the Tribulation may be *saved by faith, keep the testimony of Jesus* (12:17), and have *adequate works* to retain his salvation, but the moment he gives in to temptation and receives that mark, he is *dead lost.* **"Any"** means any in Revelation 14:9. A person could believe like the Phillipian jailer, be baptized like the Ethiopian eunuch, and follow the Law like John the Baptist and *loose it all by taking the mark.* This alone proves salvation then will be little like it is today.

Even with this faith and works setup great multitudes will refuse to take the mark, and, as a result, most of them will be killed (13:15, 20:4). Motivated be jealously and pride, the Beast will slaughter believers wholesale (13:7) with no restraint, but even this will not hinder yet others from **"the faith of Jesus."** Also, during this time there will be 144,000 Jewish "missionaries" sealed and protected by God preaching the gospel of the kingdom (not the gospel of the grace of God) and two witnesses (most likely Moses and Elijah) performing signs and wonders and declaring the truth to the world. It will be a drastically different situation than it is today. Then it will more often than not cost one a great deal to be saved, likely even his life! Nevertheless, many will **"love not their lives unto death"** and refuse to blaspheme God by taking the mark. Like James said, they will show their faith by their works (Jam. 2:18).

In a nutshell salvation in the Tribulation will be obtained and secured by *having faith in Jesus as Savior and Messiah, keeping the commandments and doing what one knows to be right, and avoiding the mark of the beast at all costs.* Failure to do these things and endure faithfully to the end *can cost a person everything he has gained.* Many today teach Church Age believers will go through the Tribulation. If so according to Revelation 14 they can lose their salvation by taking the mark.

As we have said, the typical Fundamentalist method of dealing with Tribulation salvation is to pretend it is identical to salvation today. But unfortunately, many Baptists and Fundamentalists are much more loyal to their pet "historic positions" than to the Bible. They utterly refuse to take the verses as they stand. They will not hesitate to *twist, distort, wrest, spiritualize,* and *"Greekify"* these plain verses to make them conform to their doctrine. The author says this being a Baptist and Fundamentalist himself, however, his allegiance is to the Scriptures alone and not some "historic Baptist position." He has found from reading Fundamentalist material that some Baptist doctrines are just as much heresy as those of Mormons and Jehovah's Witnesses. The only real difference between the heretical Baptist doctrines and those of the cults is the lies of the cults are lethal to the soul while the "positions" of the Fundamentalists are lethal to dispensational truth.

You may be thinking, "You say most Baptists are wrong on Tribulation salvation, but I am not convinced." Good, neither this book nor any other like it should settle doctrinal matters in the mind of any believer. Only one book is to do this and every Christian's duty is to search it out and determine what it says. If you want to know the truth get in the BOOK! Never mind the commentators when they refuse to believe it. God expects every believer to search the Scriptures and study them out *personally* for himself and learn Bible doctrine first hand (Acts 17:11). Preachers, sermons, commentators and teachers all have their place, but they are no substitute for personal study of the Scriptures.

The Millennium And Beyond

After the mass death and destruction of the Tribulation and second coming of Christ, there will be relatively few people left on the earth. There will be a certain number of Jews from each tribe left to inherit the land promised to Abraham, and also a number of Gentiles who didn't take the mark to dwell in other areas, but compared to today the earth's population will be much reduced. In many respects man will have a fresh start. As mentioned in chapter 1, The Millennium will be the fulfillment of the Kingdom of Heaven Christ preached to the Jews at the beginning of His ministry (Matt. 3).

In the "sermon on the mount" Christ declared the principles and doctrines of this kingdom to the Jews and all they had to do to receive it was repent as a nation and receive Jesus as their Messiah and King. Of course they did not do this and in the end they even killed their Messiah, but the offer of the kingdom was nonetheless valid. After murdering their promised King, the offer of the kingdom was postponed until Israel repents and is willing to receive the one they slew. God was merciful towards them and gave them more opportunities to repent in the book of Acts, but Israel again vehemently refused. We now know they won't get right until Revelation chapter 20. It is the same kingdom described in Matthew chapters 5-7 only postponed for at least 2000 years.

The Sermon on the Mount tells us a great deal about the doctrines that will be valid during the Millennium, and one reading should convince any unbiased reader that they are based on WORKS. Faith and belief in God are not even mentioned. In the kingdom one can be tried by a judicial council for calling his brother **"Raca"** and be cast into Hell for calling him a **"fool"** (5:22)! He can be judged as a adulterer for only lusting after someone (5:28) and be judged as a murderer for entertaining hate. Then it will be profitable for a person to cut off parts of his body if it will keep him from doing wrong works (5:29-30)! Cutting off his hand may keep him out of Hell! Is that not what the verses say? See how "obscure," "unclear," and "difficult" verses clear up when they are rightly divided and kept in their proper context?

A lost person today could cut off every member of his body and it wouldn't keep him out of Hell one second, but in the Millennium it may keep him out for eternity. Today one must be born again, but not so in the Millennium. The problem most Christians have with passages like Matthew 5:29-30 is not that they can't understand them, *it is that they can't BELIEVE them.* They readily receive clear and easy verses like John 3:16, but verses like this are hard for them to swallow. The problem is not in "interpretation" but in believing. Actually, very little of the Bible needs to be interpreted; it only needs to be believed.

During the Millennium Christ will be personally reigning over the entire earth from the throne of David in Jerusalem (Zech. 14:9). He will rule with a **"rod of iron"** enforcing His law of righteousness upon all and judging those who rebel (Matthew 5:22). Since Christ will be physically on earth, no one then needs to have faith that He exists or wonder if He can do what He has promised. All those who make it through the Tribulation will see Him for who He really is, **"God manifest in the flesh."** Therefore in the Millennium faith will not be the deciding factor in a person receiving salvation, obedience will be the key. Furthermore, preaching the **"gospel"** and witnessing to the "lost" will be nonexistent. In fact, Zechariah 13:2 says anyone who does preach or prophesy will be killed! Also, there will be no place for evangelism because everyone (at least all Jews) will know the Lord (Heb. 8:11).

The Jews who enter in from the Tribulation will be saved, but they can lose their salvation if they fail to work or perform evil works. The **"sheep"** (Gentiles, Matt. 25) who enter in will also be saved, but they can lose their salvation the same way, too. Another group will be those born during the Millennium and they will have to be saved once they are old enough to understand. Faith may have a part with their initial salvation, but, nevertheless, from then on they must work to keep it. This is where the "beatitudes" come in. There is no mention of faith in the Beatitudes; they deal solely with works. It is a work to be **"poor in spirit"** when man by nature is not. Likewise it is work to **"mourn,"** be **"meek,"** to **"hunger and thirst after righteousness,"** be **"merciful,"** be **"pure in heart,"** and a **"peacemaker."** The obvious domination of this passage by works is the reason it is used by Modernists and Liberals to teach salvation by works today. They understand what the verses say, they just apply them to the wrong people. "Today's heresy is tomorrow's truth," and, again, the difference is in the dispensations.

Like those saved in the Old Testament and the Tribulation period, no one in the Millennium will be born again, part of the body of Christ, partakers of the divine nature, sealed by the Holy Spirit, etc. Individuals will have only their old Adamic nature and will be saved by faith and works on a trial basis with works now being the major component. With the lack of works or the wrong works one could quickly find himself in Hell. Also, during the kingdom there will be a temple (Eze. 40-48) in Jerusalem and animal sacrifices will again be offered pointing back to the cross. All people from every nation will be required to come to Jerusalem and worship Christ and keep the feast of tabernacles (Zech. 14:16). Does this sound like the "Church Age"?

Another group of people in the Millennium will be the **"Bride of Christ"** who went up in the rapture at least seven years earlier. As mentioned in chapter 1, all believers who make up the Body of Christ will have a glorified, resurrection body like Christ's and be literally dead unto sin; that is, unable to sin. They will then have only the righteous nature of Christ. Apparently, born again Christians will be Christ's ministers or ambassadors, doing His bidding throughout the Kingdom (Rev. 20:4). This is also the period referred to in 1 Corinthians 6:2 where Christians are said to judge Angels. Furthermore, there is good indication that some Old Testament saints will be resurrected to enjoy the Millennium. Abraham, Isaac, and Jacob are said to be in the Kingdom of Heaven (Matt. 8:11) as well as David (Eze. 34:23-24) and Job (Job 19:25-27). Many more, if not all, Old Testament believers may be raised up to partake of the promised kingdom. Those that are will be dead to sin just like those saved in the Church Age, but they will not be part of the Body of Christ.

The Satanic revolt at the end of the Millennium will likely be peopled by those who were born during the Millennium (the **"children of the kingdom"** Matt. 8:12?) since they never experienced the Tribulation or the consequences of sin unrestrained. Satan will surely capitalize on their pride and ignorance to fuel his last diabolical charge against God — then God will consume them all (Rev. 20).

The New Heavens And New Earth

After the Millennium, renovation of the earth by fire, and the White Throne Judgment, God will establish *a New Heavens, a new Earth,* and a *New Jerusalem* (Rev. 21:1-2). Clearly the New Heaven is for the saved *Gentiles,* the New Earth for the *Jews,* and the New Jerusalem for the *Body of Christ* (21:9). The three distinct groups of people mentioned in 1 Corinthians 10:32 are apparently established as groups for eternity with separate places of abode. The New Jerusalem like the old Jerusalem will be the dwelling place of God and house His throne forever. This city is the Christians Heaven, actually the **"third Heaven,"** and when it descends to earth Christ in all His glory will come with it and dwell in the midst of His bride for all eternity. The city will radiate with the glory of God (vs. 11) and have no need of the sun. Also, it will contain no temple because God Himself will be present, finally dwelling among His redeemed creation as He desires.

The concept of the Tabernacle in the wilderness revealed to Moses 3500 years ago gave man the first indication of the desire of God to dwell in the midst of His people. It is amazing to think that the infinite God of Heaven would chose to dwell in a tent in a wilderness just so He could be near His people! *How much He desired their company,* but they didn't desire His. Likewise, how much must God love born again Christians that He is willing to *dwell inside each individual's body just so He can have true fellowship with him.* Yet, sadly, most seldom take advantage of His presence and usually live like He is not even there! Anyway, in the 4500 years following the revealing of His desires to Moses, God devised a redemption plan and placed those who believed in and accepted His redemption in a position in which He could dwell in and among them for eternity. No one can enter this city except their name be found written in the **"book of life"** (21:27) or are found worthy to partake of the **"tree of life"** (22:14).

As for the Jew, the earth will belong to the Jew. The meek were promised the earth in the "Sermon on the Mount," and this is fulfilled with the New Earth. The Jews who don't revolt against Christ in the Millennium and make it through the White Throne Judgment appear to inherit *the whole earth.* Likewise the Gentiles appear to get the *heavens with all the stars and planets.* When dealing with things in or near eternity we admit certain matters are hard to pin down. There are many details about this "period" which are not yet revealed and hard to be certain about. For one, there is no verse that mentions the Jews or Gentiles getting a new body, so it is possible there will still have their "repaired" natural bodies at least until they eat of the **"tree of life."** In natural bodies the Jews can reproduce and fill the earth, and likewise the Gentiles can populate outer space. They may even be able to reproduce after they eat of the **"tree of life"** but the condition of their offspring is uncertain. Whether their offspring would be born with eternal life or have to eat of the tree themselves is unknown. One thing for certain, however, is that to obtain eternal life then one is not to "believe" in anything or have "faith" in anybody. He is to only keep the commandments of God so he may eat of the **"tree of life."**

Those saved in the Tribulation and Millennium will likely have to eat of this tree also to get eternal life since the new birth was unavailable to them. With the privilege of eating from this tree based entirely upon works there is always the possibility of failure, and those who fail must be cast out (21:27). Nevertheless, none of this will affect the Bride of Christ in any way. They are permanently secure and each individual received eternal life the instant he received Christ. No Christian will ever need to eat of the **"tree of life"** to get or keep eternal life, but those saved in other dispensations and not in Christ must eat of the tree to get it. See the difference? You, if you are saved, did not get eternal life from any tree, you got it from a PERSON, Jesus Christ, the Author of life. But after the rapture no one will be a part of Christ as a Christian is, thus he must have eternal life imparted another way. Check the verses! What do they say? The difference is in the dispensations.

Of the three groups of people in eternity only one is *fixed* in number (the Church), and the others will have the job of increasing the kingdom (Isa. 9:6-7). The Jews will expand and cover the earth, and maybe beyond, and the Gentiles will begin on earth but then multiply and cover the universe. Ever wonder why the stars and planets are in the heavens? There is good indication they were put there for more than just man to look at. It appears God will populate them with men who love Him and desire to serve Him. Both Jews and Gentiles that are found worthy will have to come into New Jerusalem to the life giving trees that border the river and eat of them to get the blessing of eternal life. God has come full circle. Time began with man and a tree, and it ends with man and a tree; but in the meanwhile God showed man what kind of *gracious, merciful, loving God He is.* Without man's fall and God's redemption, no one would ever know!

A Final Word

We are well aware that the position we take concerning salvation in the dispensations is controversial, and we may even be branded as a heretic because of it, but our duty to the Scriptures remains. We contend that the Scriptures must be taken as they stand and not twisted to support any popular "historic position." Of course we could use the typical Baptist method of handling verses like Matthew chapters 5-7; 24:13-15; chapter 25; Hebrews 3:6, 13-14; 6:1-6; 10:26-31; 12:14-15; James chapter 2, 5:1-5, 11-20; 2 Peter 2:21-22, 3:17; Revelation 3:5, 12:17, 13:7, 14:9-12, 22:14; etc. (not to mention all the Old Testament verses!), and insist theses verses don't really mean what they say and must be "interpreted" or "explained" to understand them, but we will no longer do that. By Christ's strength our allegiance is to God and His book (AV 1611), and when any *doctrine, teaching,* or *position* runs contrary to what God has revealed in His book, God help us to recognize it and abandon it. We believe the Bible is to be taken literally wherever possible (else one could "interpret" the Scriptures to say whatever he wanted), and when the above verses are taken literally, all is clear, *somebody* can lose their salvation. But, again, it is NOT a born again Christian.

Some may think this whole matter is irrelevant since everyone who is saved today is saved by faith alone and is secure in Christ, but they are misguided. Christ said man lives **"by every word that proc-cedeth out of the mouth of God"** so every word in the Bible is *relevant, important,* and *alive.* Though Christians are not under the Law of Moses and will not have to endure to the end like those in the Tribulation, the knowledge that some will endure those things helps believers today better understand what God is doing. Bible believers have a great advantage over believers who fail to treat the Bible literally. They have an excellent picture of the *past, present,* and *future* from God's perspective as He has revealed it. God very much wants His people to know *where they came from, the state they are in now, and where they are going,* else He wouldn't have given this revelation. And though God's revelation admitingly has some sometimes perplexing differences found among it pages, one is usually able to make sense of them when he realizes that most often, *the difference is in the dispen-sations.*

The Covenants

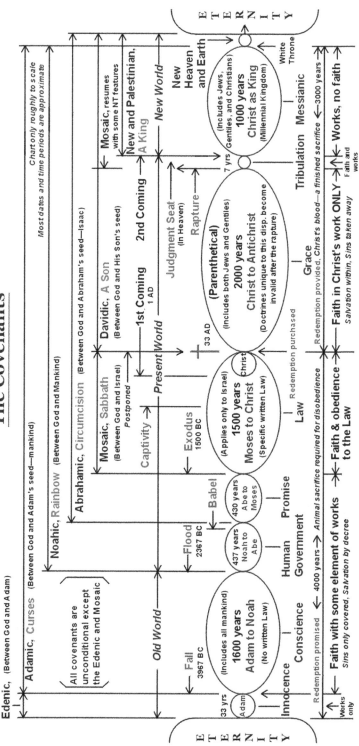

Edenic, (Between God and Adam)

Adamic, Curses (Between God and Adam's seed—mankind)

Noahic, Rainbow (Between God and Mankind)

Abrahamic, Circumcision (Between God and Abraham's seed—mankind)

Mosaic, Sabbath (Between God and Israel)

Davidic, A Son (Between God and Abraham's seed—Isaac)

Mosaic, resumes with some NT features

New and Palestinian, A King

All covenants are unconditional except the Edenic and Mosaic

Chart only roughly to scale
Most dates and time periods are approximate

Old World

Fall
3967 BC

(Includes all mankind)
1600 years
Adam to Noah
(No written Law)

Flood
2367 BC

437 years
Noah to Abe

Babel

430 years
Abe to Moses

(Applies only to Israel)
1500 years
Moses to Christ
(Specific written Law)

Exodus
1500 BC

Captivity

Present World

1st Coming
1 AD

33 AD

Christ

Postponed

Judgment Seat
(In Heaven)

Rapture

2nd Coming

New World

(Parenthetical)
(Includes both Jews and Gentiles)
2000 years
Christ to Antichrist
(Doctrines unique to this disp. become invalid after the rapture)

7 yrs

New Heaven and Earth

(Includes Jews, Gentiles, and Christians)
1000 years
Christ as King
(Millennial Kingdom)

White Throne

33 yrs   Adam

Redemption purchased

E T E R N I T Y

E T E R N I T Y

The Dispensations

Innocence | Conscience | Human Government | Promise | Law | Grace | Tribulation | Messianic

Redemption promised ←— 4000 years —→ Animal sacrifice required for disobedience → Redemption provided, Christ's blood—a finished sacrifice ←—3000 years —→

Works only → Faith with some element of works → Faith & obedience to the Law → Faith in Christ's work ONLY → Works, no faith

Sins only covered, Salvation by decree | Salvation within, Sins taken away | Faith and works

From, "The Difference is in the Dispensations."

© Timothy S. Morton, 1993, 2000

103

Made in United States
North Haven, CT
28 December 2021

13762595R00065